Praises for *Living Through the Struggle*

"As a man who has faced much suffering throughout his life, Pastor Chad Nightingale is well-positioned to interact with the teachings found in Peter's first epistle. *Living Through the Struggle* is not a commentary on 1 Peter; rather, it is a guide to application based on Peter's letter. Peppered with interesting personal stories, and ending each chapter with thought-provoking questions, Nightingale draws readers into the text to examine their lives in light of God's Word. The book will prove valuable for both personal and small-group Bible study."

Gary E. Gilley, Senior Pastor, Southern View Chapel, Springfield, Illinois

---

"Theologically true, Scripturally sound, and written from a pastor's perspective. Timely and personal; the thought-provoking questions make this is a good personal read as well as a great resource to use with small groups."

Rich McCarrell, D.D., Executive Director, IMI/SOS

"When Chad Nightingale writes about living through the struggle, he does so with experience and understanding. Not only has he navigated through difficult places by applying the principles of 1 Peter himself, he has helped countless others to do the same. Although his book cannot provide a magic formula to remove suffering, it does offer practical guidance on bringing glory to God through suffering to those who are courageous enough to live in obedience under the pressure that suffering brings."

Jimmy Van Dyck, National Administrator at Encounter Revival Ministries

---

"Chad Nightingale takes students of the Bible on a personal journey that prepares believers for and explains hardship in life. His guide is insightful, clear, and concise. Through reflective questions, readers consider in detail marriage, work relationships, and faithfulness. We all want to live well, but Nightingale directs readers to the truths that help us accomplish that task. I highly recommend this tool for personal devotions or intimate small-group study."

Victor "Skip" Hessel, Jr., D.M., Graduate School Dean, Business Administration Department Chair, Organization Development Program Director, Calvary University

"In an effort to point to the glorious realities of a new life in Christ, some versions of the gospel have actually downplayed the reality of continuing difficulties, trials, and persecution in the life of every believer. Becoming a Christian does not remove all of a person's problems, but instead points us to the finished work of Christ, which is sufficient to equip us for facing life with our Savior. Chad Nightingale's book looks at this important reality through the epistle of 1 Peter. Pastor Nightingale writes with clarity and pastoral concern as he not only explains the main ideas in Peter's letter, but also helps readers by giving thoughtful application questions so we can apply Scripture to the heart. *Living Through the Struggle* is a wonderful resource for the struggling soul."

Dr. Richard Bargas, Executive Director, IFCA International, and editor, The VOICE magazine

---

"I am thrilled to recommend Chad Nightingale, because I know firsthand that he has been used by God in many ways to help others with their spiritual needs. I know that you will be encouraged by this book on trouble. As you follow the Biblical examples that he suggests, your life will be blessed by God. Chad's faithfulness to the Word of God and his desire to obey the Lord are great reasons to recommend this work."

Ardy Parlin, founder and Director, Encounter Revival Ministries

LIVING
THROUGH THE
STRUGGLE
1 Peter's Lessons for Today

CHAD NIGHTINGALE

LARKSPUR, COLORADO

Grace Acres Press
PO Box 22
Larkspur, CO 80118
www.GraceAcresPress.com

Grace Acres Press also publishes books in a variety of electronic formats. Some content that appears in print may not be available in electronic books.

Scripture quotations are from the ESV® Bible (The Holy Bible, English Standard Version®), copyright © 2001 by Crossway, a publishing ministry of Good News Publishers. Used by permission. All rights reserved.

Print ISBN: 978-1-60265-068-8
E-book ISBN: 978-1-60265-069-5

Library of Congress Control Number:

Printed in United States of America
25 24 23 22 21 20   01 02 03 04 05 06 07 08

To my mom, Cheri J. Nightingale, who proved
you can live well in the midst of suffering.

CONTENTS

INTRODUCTION

Suffering! That is what takes place in our world. Suffering does not care about social status, economic superiority, or culture. Everyone faces suffering at some point in their lives. While Jesus was here among us, He suffered in incredible ways and provided His disciples with an example of how to do that well. He did this suffering well even when He died for us on the cross. In his first epistle to the church suffering throughout Rome, Peter explained to us, through the inspiration of God, the things that he learned while walking with Jesus.

At the age of 29, in the year 2006, after the birth of my middle son Henry, my wife, Tracy, and I heard those noise-deadening words from my doctor, "You have a malignancy." These words were followed by a long trip home from the Mayo Clinic and a year of nights in the emergency room with surgical complications, unmanageable pain, infections, and weakness. That year, and the complications which followed, changed my life dramatically. Before 2006, I was an ambitious pastor who was determined to change the world for Christ (and—let's be honest—make a name for myself in the process). After 2006, I realized that life was less about what we do or accomplish and more about how we live. This realization transformed my library from a collection of leadership and development books to a steady diet of books helping me to grow in my understanding of life lived with God. Suffering went from being a nuisance I had to deal with to a tool used in my life for the establishment of a more intimate relationship with Jesus. Peter, maybe more than any other New Testament character, allows us to understand that being with Jesus in the difficult circumstances of life is much better than finding greatness apart from Him. Peter helps us to see that we are called to live this life we have been given well even if the life we have been given is not the one we thought, hoped, or wished we would have.

In case you are wondering: No, the cancer is not gone. No, there is not a cure. And at this point, because the disease I have is so rare, not many people are looking for a cure. Like many in my family who have this disease, it will be with me for my entire life. We are going to spend many nights in the hospital, have surgeries, make trips for testing while wondering what the year ahead will look like, have children and wonder if they carry the gene. We do these things even though we already know what will most likely kill us some day.

However, everyone is terminal. Every one of us must decide how best to live this life so that if this year is the last one, we will have lived it well.

As a follower of Christ Jesus, I have had to suffer — sometimes because of my own foolishness, at other times because this world is broken and until Christ returns this suffering will continue. During the suffering I have faced, the Lord has provided many who came alongside me and guided me in how to suffer well. Those who were helpful had one thing in common: they always brought me to Scripture for the direction that would carry me through. This book is my attempt to do the same for you.

1 Peter was written to the suffering follower of Christ. My hope is that while you study Peter's letter, with your Bible open, and

read through my (hopefully helpful) illustrations, commentary, and questions, you will find the strength to bring glory to God through your suffering while waiting for the day when our Lord fulfills His promise to us and ends the suffering forever.

1

Your Struggle Is Not a Surprise

1 Peter 1:1–2:

Peter, an apostle of Jesus Christ, To those who are elect exiles of the Dispersion in Pontus, Galatia, Cappadocia, Asia, and Bithynia, (2) according to the foreknowledge of God the Father, in the sanctification of the Spirit, for obedience to Jesus Christ and for sprinkling with his blood: May grace and peace be multiplied to you.

━━━━━━━━━━━━━━━━━━━━━━━━━━

Smells bring back memories. Some of those memories are pleasant, but more often those memories are of things I wish I could forget. It is hard when odors bring back memories of struggle: Struggles that were unacceptable. Struggles that were the result of failures or mistakes. Struggles that I did not see coming. Struggles that I thought would somehow turn out differently.

Like me, I'm sure you have had your share of struggles. Would you allow me to encourage you for a few moments with this simple little truth? God knew your struggle was coming. He made it part of His plan and He is using it to shape you into the person He designed you to be.

The Human Instrument Used to Write the First Epistle of Peter

Who is Peter? He is the one who:

- Proclaimed Christ as God (Mark 8:27–29).

- Walked on water (Matt. 14:22–33).

- Saw the miracles (Luke 7 [for one]).

- Refused to accept the possibility of Jesus' death (Matt. 16:21–23).

- Stood against guards when they tried to take Jesus away (John 18:10).

- Denied Jesus three times while Jesus was on trial (John 18:15–27).

- Ran to see that Jesus had risen (Luke 24:12).

- Christ personally asked to care for the church (John 21:15–19).

- Was challenged by changes in the church that went against tradition and yet surrendered to Christ (Acts 10; 15:6 11).

- After being beaten by soldiers, called it a privilege to suffer for the name of Christ (Acts 5:40–41).

- Died graciously on a cross, probably upside down because he believed he was unworthy to die in the same manner as his Lord.

What do we learn from Peter's life?

- God has a better understanding of what brings good than even His most dedicated followers.

- God does not need an individual to be perfect to use that individual for His good.

- Surrender to Christ does not mean life will be enjoyable.

The Original Audience of Peter's Letter

Peter wrote to followers of Jesus Christ who had been redeemed through the power of His blood, living without citizenship because their home had been taken from them. Citizenship in Rome was a rare privilege (Acts 22:25–28). Scripture only tells us that the wealthy could purchase this privilege, and that it was given to individuals born in a free province (provincials). "The provincials were people from the provinces who were under Roman control or influence, but who only had basic rights under international law (*ius gentium*). Freedmen were former slaves who had gained their freedom and were not automatically given Roman citizenship. Their children, however, were born free citizens" (www.romae-vitam.com). This difficulty in becoming a citizen created a separate class of people.

Peter wrote to individuals under the care of an all-powerful, all-knowing, everpresent God. The redemption of these individuals was not a surprise to God. Nor was their present situation (Ps. 139). God allowed their location, situation, and the struggle they found themselves in because that was the perfect setting for their spiritual growth (1 Thess. 4:1–8). They understood that growth in their spiritual walk included separation from immorality and dying to the constant temptations of the flesh. It meant yielding control of their lives to Christ.

Peter wrote to these individuals who had been positioned to live in obedience to Christ, demonstrating with an outward response the inward changes that were taking place (1 Peter 1:14, 22). In obedience they cast off the things that once possessed their lives, laying aside the temptations of this world, and being possessed by Jesus Christ who saved their souls.

The individuals Peter wrote to were established as righteous before God (Heb. 10:19–25). They approached God with confidence, being assured that they had a perfect living high priest in heaven. They also knew that their security lay not in their own performance, but in Christ alone, who was their hope, and nothing else. Because of this, they encouraged one another in worshipping, praying, and assembling together. In all, Peter wrote to believers who lived in a world that dismissed the things they were most passionate about as trivial religious practices, niceties, or offensively divisive ideas.

What Makes This Epistle Helpful to Us?

Peter acknowledged the struggles of those to whom he wrote. It is helpful to understand that God chose the pen of a man who suffered much, failed big time, and—through Christ—finished well to bring this to us. It is a reminder that we are not alone in our suffering and God will not waste it, providing for us a way to live in this world to the praise, honor, and glory of Christ. All of this is helpful when confronting suffering, knowing that the world is looking for almost any reason to persecute us.

This present world is a difficult place. Walking with Christ through the transformation only He can bring is not easy, but it is the best and only journey that leads to our becoming who God intended us to be.

?≡ Responding to God's Word in our lives:

- What kind of difficult situation are you facing in your life?

- In what way do you think God is able to use that situation to transform you into the person He wants you to be?

- Are you willing to place yourself in His care as you walk through these difficult days?

- Are you willing to submit to His ways when they may seem contrary to your own intuition?

- Are you, like Peter, willing to quit leading yourself and allow God to lead you where you were not willing to go before (John 21:18)?

2

In Suffering Our Faith Is Given Sustenance

1 Peter 1:3–9:

Blessed be the God and Father of our Lord Jesus Christ! According to his great mercy, he has caused us to be born again to a living hope through the resurrection of Jesus Christ from the dead, (4) to an inheritance that is imperishable, undefiled, and unfading, kept in heaven for you, (5) who by God's power are being guarded through faith for a salvation ready to be revealed in the last time. (6) In this you rejoice, though now for a little while, if necessary, you have been grieved by various trials, (7) so that the tested genuineness of your faith—more precious than gold that perishes though it is tested by fire—may be found to result in praise and glory and honor at the revelation of Jesus Christ. (8) Though you have not seen him, you love him. Though you do not now see him, you believe in him and rejoice with joy that is inexpressible and filled with glory, (9) obtaining the outcome of your faith, the salvation of your souls.

It is unfortunate that material prosperity, obtained or achieved without understanding the cost, often leads to spoiled children who turn into spoiled adults. This is as clearly seen in the church today as anywhere else within a prosperous nation. We live thinking that we deserve the life we have been given. We live thinking that those who do not prosper as we have are doing something wrong. We live thinking that God is lucky to have us. We live thinking that we deserve the things we have.

The thing that brings us back to reality is suffering. When we suffer, we begin to see that Jesus is more than a key to our personal chest of blessings. Instead, we see Him as we always should have: as the Lord of the universe who suffered to bring us salvation. Without suffering, we behave like spoiled children who think they know everything, including how everyone else should live their lives. When suffering becomes a part of our lives and the material things around us become useless and unreliable, we are forced to recognize what our faith is in.

Let's begin by putting our focus where it should be and making sure our thinking is correct. Remember that God deserves our adoration. God does not need our adoration, but we need to worship Him. This need to worship God and give Him our adoration requires that we put aside our own difficult situations.

Remember, too, that our redemption is the result of His mercy and not our worthiness. *Mercy* is defined as "compassion or forgiveness shown toward someone whom it is within one's power to punish or harm" (Oxford English Dictionary, 2018). Because we were living for ourselves and led by our passions, we were guilty of disobedience to God (Eph. 2:1–7). Therefore, we deserve whatever wrath God chooses to pour out on us. However, God poured out that wrath that we deserved on Christ so that in surrendering to Him, we would be saved from that wrath.

God's act of mercy has transformed us from individuals without hope to persons who live in hope. As recipients of God's merciful gift, it becomes our responsibility to grow in our understanding of the hope that is within us (Eph. 1:15–21). We should seize the power God has given to us and search out the inheritance that we have. Our lives should be spent dwelling in this hope, which is given by grace through faith. We were once dead to our spiritual life, but we have been given new life, free from the control of sin.

Our hope is the result of Jesus' death overcoming power (1 Cor. 15:17–19). Our reward is an eternal righteousness that can never be taken from us. This is the doctrine of eternal security. It reminds us that we will receive what has been promised through faith; nothing will take that from us. It reminds us that the righteousness we have been given is not our own. The blessings we have through eternal security sustain us when we fail, strengthen us when we are weak, and prepare us for our day of judgment.

When we cannot find joy in anything else, we find it in what Jesus Christ did for us on the cross. We cling to our redemption in Christ because the difficulties of this life can bring us to despair. We also cling to our redemption in Christ to prove to the enemies of Christ that we are His. When we endure the difficulties of this life obediently, Jesus is praised, He is glorified, and His name is lifted up.

The outward manifestation of our obedience to Christ is evidence of our inner faith. As believers, we are surrendered to the desire of One we have not seen. We look forward to the return of Christ confidently because of His promise to return. Even when the physical body cannot respond because of injury or disease, we rejoice in our hearts. Our security lies in the promise of a faithful God who has never failed to fulfill His Word.

Believers are secure in the salvation offered to everyone and anyone who will believe on their need for a Savior, the Lord Jesus Christ. Jesus left heaven and lived a sinless life. His surrender on the cross was to take the weight of God's wrath toward sinners upon Himself. He rose again to demonstrate His power over death and empower believers to grow in Him through the Holy Spirit. Believers have His righteousness that was established by the shedding of His blood, and allows us to live securely in His promises.

?≡   **Responding to God's Word in our lives:**

Have you called upon the name of the Lord Jesus for salvation? You can do that today, right now. You do not have to continue in the course you are on. But only you can decide to follow Jesus. Here is how you call upon the name of Jesus for salvation:

- By faith in what Jesus has done for us on the cross (Eph. 2:8–9).

- Admit to God that you are a sinner without hope of salvation except through the shed blood of Jesus Christ, which is received by faith (Rom. 3:21–25).

- Acknowledge that your sin qualifies you for judgment in hell eternally separated from God (1 Cor. 6:9–10).

- Ask God to forgive your sin based on the death Jesus endured for you on the cross (Rom. 5:8–10).

- Turn from living in disobedience to God and walk with Jesus in the new life provided by His resurrection from the dead (Gal. 5:16–26).

- If you have asked Jesus Christ to be your Savior, then consider how you are living. Are you clinging to the hope we have and surrendering yourself to His transforming process, or are you continuing to live as though you were not transformed by His power?

- In what ways does your life reflect an individual surrendered to the transforming power of Jesus Christ?

- What areas of your life should change because they are not a reflection of the transforming power of Jesus Christ?

3
A Message Worth Suffering For

1 Peter 1:10–12:
Concerning this salvation, the prophets who prophesied about the grace that was to be yours searched and inquired carefully, (11) inquiring what person or time the Spirit of Christ in them was indicating when he predicted the sufferings of Christ and the subsequent glories. (12) It was revealed to them that they were serving not themselves but you, in the things that have now been announced to you through those who preached the good news to you by the Holy Spirit sent from heaven, things into which angels long to look.

I have a great affection for ice cream and pizza. Truthfully, there was a time when I could have eaten one or both every day and I would not have grown tired of either. As I passed the 40-year-old mark, my body determined I should not eat either of these on a regular basis. Now when I look at the ice-cream section while my wife looks at the healthier side of the grocery aisle, I have to ask if sneaking a couple half-gallons of ice cream into the shopping cart will be worth the upset stomach that will follow my evening snack. These days I must admit that often the consequences outweigh the temporal pleasure of "Tin Roof Sundae."

For most of my life, it has been easy—even popular—to say I was a pastor or member of a local Bible-believing church. For politicians, it was a way of gaining credibility. For businesspeople, it was a means of building a client base. This was true because claiming to be a Christian did not carry consequences like it is beginning to today. In our current cultural climate, being a Christian is not an asset, especially being a Christian who believes the Bible is always true and provides the instructions by which a person must live to be saved. Now we are put in a position in which we must ask ourselves if being a follower of Christ is worth what it will cost us.

What is it we know about this salvation we have been given? We know the Kingdom established by Christ will go on for all eternity (Dan. 2:44). We know the cross of Christ is not a passing ideology. We know it is and always has been, since eternity past, the basis of God's plan for this world.

The cost of our salvation was already revealed by the prophets (Luke 24:25–27). Jesus died because there wasn't another way, there was no other option. Knowing this is true does not mean we have to fight with every person who does not believe the gospel message of the Bible. Nevertheless, we must challenge the thinking that there are multiple correct answers. There is only one right answer. To follow Christ is to let everything you have rest on the reality of His gospel as that one right answer.

There will be a day when this salvation will be acknowledged by all and total obedience to Christ will be established through it (Gen. 49:10). One day every knee will bow before Christ. There is not a question as to whether you will bow. There is a question as to whether you will bow in awe and majesty before your Savior, or you will bow begging for a forgiveness that is no longer available.

The prophets knew what they were looking for because they sought to find instruction and understanding from the Word of God (Prov. 2:4). As followers of Jesus, we must become like the prophets. We cannot be satisfied with a basic knowledge of God. We need to pursue an understanding of Christ as individuals who have everything to gain from this pursuit—because we do.

When the prophets spoke, they were not speaking on their own behalf; rather, through the power of the Holy Spirit, they uttered the perfect Word of God (2 Peter 1:19–21). When we surrender, it is not as if we do so to the opinions of clever speakers. Our interest is in the infallible Word of God.

They proclaimed salvation by faith in Christ for the forgiveness of sins (Acts 10:43). This is not a new idea. The inability of the law to save is not a surprise. The proving of Scripture is our total inability to save ourselves. Individuals who think they are saved by anything other than the blood of Christ are fooling themselves and will bear the eternal consequences of that foolishness.

Every prophet proclaimed the coming of Christ as a subject of supreme importance, and they encouraged all to listen to His instruction (Acts 3:22–24). Furthermore, they pronounced the destruction of all who disregard His words.

These prophets, devoted servants of God, were not embraced by the people of Israel or the rulers of Israel. In fact, the prophets were killed for their proclamation of the coming Christ (Acts 7:52). It is foolish to think that our task will make us loved by those who reject Christ. We must make sure it is not our cantankerous, hypocritical, or know-it-all attitude that is being rejected rather than the message we are called to give. We must be careful to make sure it is the message they hate, and not the way that message is given. The gospel is honorable, but it will be despised by those who reject Christ. A poor testimony of bad behavior becomes a stain on the message of the gospel and the church of God.

Those who brought the message of salvation to us died steadfast in the message they proclaimed (Heb. 11:13, 11:40). The prophets knew exactly what the Christ would do. They knew how and where He would be born and what He would do in ministry. They knew ahead of time that He would be rejected by the Jews. His suffering, crucifixion, and resurrection were also foretold. They knew He was victorious. What they didn't know was exactly when this would all take place.

We know that the events the prophets predicted came true (Gen. 3:15). We know that the events still to come will take place (Gen. 49:10). As a result we do not proclaim anything but what the prophets have given (John 12:41). Like the prophets, we live and proclaim Christ, not for our own good, but for the good of others.

Because of this, we must get over ourselves and submit to the needs of others. This work that God is doing in the world is not boring. The task that we have been called to in the work of the gospel has the attention of angels in heaven. The gospel of Christ is worth suffering for. The question each of us must ask is whether we are willing to pay the price, so others may be saved. What rights should we willingly give up in order to reach a lost world with the gospel of Jesus Christ?

?≡ Responding to God's Word in our lives:

If we have not accepted the gospel of salvation, we are missing the whole point of our existence here.

- Have you believed Jesus Christ is the Savior we all need?

- If not, what is keeping you from doing that?

- If we are not taking part in the spreading of the gospel, then we are not involved in what God is doing in this world. What are some ways in which you can spread the gospel to others?

There is nothing of lasting value in this world apart from what has been given to us in the Word of God.

- Are you spending time in God's Word?

- What is keeping you away from this?

4

Saved (Redemption) and Being Saved (Sanctification)

1 Peter 1:13–25:

Therefore, preparing your minds for action, and being sober-minded, set your hope fully on the grace that will be brought to you at the revelation of Jesus Christ. (14) As obedient children, do not be conformed to the passions of your former ignorance, (15) but as he who called you is holy, you also be holy in all your conduct, (16) since it is written, "You shall be holy, for I am holy." (17) And if you call on him as Father who judges impartially according to each one's deeds, conduct yourselves with fear throughout the time of your exile, (18) knowing that you were ransomed from the futile ways inherited from your forefathers, not with perishable things such as silver or gold, (19) but with the precious blood of Christ, like that of a lamb without blemish or spot. (20) He was foreknown before the foundation of the world but was made manifest in the last times for the sake of you (21) who through him are believers in God, who raised him from the dead and gave him glory, so that your faith and hope are in God. (22) Having purified your souls by your obedience to the truth for a sincere brotherly love, love one another earnestly from a pure heart, (23) since you have been born again, not of perishable seed but of imperishable, through the living and abiding word of God; (24) for "All flesh is like grass and all its glory like the flower of grass. The grass withers, and the flower falls, (25) but the word of the Lord remains forever." And this word is the good news that was preached to you.

Theological terms can often muddy the waters of understanding. They can be easily misused, misinterpreted, misunderstood.

This leads us to believe things that are not true, expect things of ourselves that God does not expect, and fail to participate in things that are necessary for regular spiritual growth.

When I was 16 years old, like many others, I went with my father to get a driver's license. This license gave me all the rights and responsibilities of every other driver on the road. I took the classes, passed the tests, put in my 50 hours of driving time, and I was a driver. For a short month or so, I was a little hesitant behind the wheel. I was cautious and careful because I was a little bit insecure about my abilities as a driver. In the next months I found myself pushing the limits of my abilities and often the abilities of my car. By the time I was 17 years old I believed I was, at the very least, one of the best drivers on the road. Speed limits and the possible dangers awaiting were for less effective drivers. For some reason God allowed me to survive those years until I was old enough to realize that my great effectiveness as a driver was more in my head, and maybe the hands of angels, than in my abilities.

As human beings, the cycles we go through as we develop in any area are very interesting. People go through the same pattern over and over. First is being given a role. Then comes carrying out that role—at first nervously and then with increasing bravado—until they believe wholeheartedly that they have mastered it beyond the abilities of most who have gone before them. Then, over much time and failure, they realize they are not as able, wise, or gifted as they once believed they were.

In this portion of his letter to the scattered believers, Peter provides us with a contrast between our former selves and what we have become as a result of our salvation. These are the things given as a result of Christ's blood and the transformation it has made in our lives. He then shows those things which are possible because of what Christ has done and will do in us as we surrender to His leading in our lives. It is helpful to understand our position as a result of salvation (Eph. 2:8–9) and the work that must still be done while Christ Jesus is changing us (Phil. 1:6).

First we must understand that there are automatic realities for everyone upon becoming a Christian. We have been placed into a position of heir to the kingdom of God and all its riches. We have the listening ear of God Almighty. Our everyday acts have eternal value. We are purified before God. Importantly, we have become dependent upon the Word of God for instruction and nourishment.

The instruction from the Word of God defines the transformation that should be taking place. Included in this is a mind that is focused on and not distracted from our Father's purposes. Another part of this growth is the ability to put aside our natural desires and develop an understanding of what it means to be set apart. When being transformed, we should be growing in a reverence for the God of the universe and gaining an affection for the blood of Christ.

When we can surrender to God's Word in all decisions, it creates an outpouring of love covered in truth from a heart not seeking its own good. When we surrender to Jesus Christ as our Lord and Savior, we are placed in a position we could not ever earn. We are also given the power, through the Holy Spirit, to grow closer relationally to God, from Whom we had previously been separated.

?≡ Responding to God's Word in our lives:

- Have you been placed securely in the care of Jesus Christ as the means of your salvation?

- If not, what is keeping you from making this decision?

- If you have believed on Jesus for salvation, are you participating in the resources given for your spiritual growth in sanctification?

Just as an athlete must do certain things to prepare for an event, there are things all Christians must do if they are going to grow in their relationship with Jesus. As a diagnostic tool, consider whether or not you are participating in the normal means of spiritual growth. If the answer to these queries is no, then it does not matter how spiritual you think you are; you are not growing in Christ as you should be. Remember: these things do not make you a Christian, but you will not grow as a Christian without them.

- How often do you spend time reading the Bible?

- What would be a regular pattern for your prayer life?

- How often do you take part in the regular gathering of other believers for worship, encouragement, and instruction (local church)?

- How often are you engaged with your church family for the Lord's supper (communion)?

- What relationships have you developed with other believers who challenge you with regular daily Christian living?

5

Breaking Down the Old Man

1 Peter 2:1:
So put away all malice and all deceit and hypocrisy and envy and all slander.

━━━━━━━━━━━━━━━━━━━━━━━━━━━━━━━━━

Every spring I clean out my garage. I begin this project by removing everything and putting it out on my driveway. When I have everything out, the work begins. The floor is cleaned, the shelves are dusted off, the toolboxes are put in order, and the tools are properly hung on the walls. Everything looks wonderful. Then I look at the driveway and determine what things must go back in. In all honesty, I have to say that when the bikes, travel boxes, building materials, and cleaning/yard supplies are put back into the garage, it does not look like a wonderful place. It looks more like an organized mess—one that will quickly get worse because my children will begin using their toys which I have placed in such a way that only with a very skilled hand would they ever end up that way again. But once in a while I find things that need not be returned to the garage, and when those things are disposed of, I may even be able to use it as a garage instead of a storage room.

A critical misstep in the life of those who have come to Christ Jesus for salvation is the removal of things that hinder us from growing in Christ. It does not matter how much you pursue the right things if you do not get rid of the old useless stuff. Let's look at the stuff in our lives that we want to remove and not ever put back, specifically if the desire is to grow in brotherly love. These are the things of character intolerable in the life of Christians as they pursue brotherly love.

We must begin with certain principles. It is not possible to begin new without cleaning out the old. If the desired outcome is brotherly love (v. 1:22), then we must dispose of the characteristics that ruin relationships.

Malice is a deep-seated desire to see someone else suffer. There is an illustration of this in King Saul's progression into madness. At first, King Saul loves David (1 Sam. 16:21–22). As David had success, Saul showed him favor (1 Sam. 18:5). When that success bred overshadowing fame, Saul descended into madness (1 Sam. 18:6–11). Malice is not sensible. It is madness driven by anger, jealousy, and discontent and it must be vanquished and purged from the heart of the believer, or brotherly love will be impossible.

Another character issue is deceit, which is displayed in being underhanded or fraudulent. Fearing the reaction of the people, the Jewish leaders plotted to arrest and kill Jesus deceitfully (Mark 14:1–2). When we fear how people will react to a decision or situation, we shape the situation to our advantage instead of facing them with transparency. In this way we damage relationships. Though we may get our own way, we lose the trust of those individuals, which is more valuable than the thing we were in pursuit of.

Hypocrisy is another sinful characteristic seen in those pretending to be something they are not or acting out a part (Matt. 23:27–28). It is *not* hypocritical to fail when attempting to be better than we are. It *is* hypocritical to pretend everything is fine when internally we are falling apart. Hypocrisy is clearly seen in the believer who acts religious at church and lives in sinfulness out in the marketplace.

Envy, often referred to as the green-eyed monster, is a painful or resentful awareness of an advantage enjoyed by another joined by a desire to have that same advantage (Matt. 27:18). Envy can lead us all the way to murder, and destroys those on whom we center our resentment. It is the central issue in our wars and fighting (Jas. 4:1–2). When Jesus becomes the singular priority in our lives, envy is easily removed (Matt. 6:33). Ambition, related to envy, has to take a back seat to God's perfect plan.

The utterance of false charges or misrepresentations that defame and damage another's reputation is slander (Jas. 4:11–12). When we speak to degrade another person, we place ourselves in a position as judge — and only God is judge. Therefore, we put ourselves in the position of God.

Malice, deceit, hypocrisy, envy, slander: these are the pride-rooted sins that destroy trust. They will destroy relationships forever. If these are a part of your life, then you need to cast them off. Repent! Lay these things at the cross of Christ and never pick them up again. Surrender these things to Him today. Now is the time to put an end to these relationship-killing characteristics and emotions. Today you can begin anew.

?≡   Responding to God's Word in our lives:

- Are there sin areas in your life that keep you from brotherly love?

- List those sins and determine how you will turn from them, allowing the Spirit of God to do the work that only He can do in the relationships around you.

- Follow through in caring for these things as the Spirit of God leads you.

6

Living as a Newborn Babe

1 Peter 2:2–3:
Like newborn infants, long for the pure spiritual milk, that by it you may grow up into salvation—(3) if indeed you have tasted that the Lord is good.

Scheduled feeding times, careful monitoring, measuring and weighing, doctor's appointments, nap times, preparation, teaching, and watching, are all part of helping our children grow. As they grow, their ability to care for themselves, determine when they should eat, and get themselves moving in the morning grows with them. Their likes and dislikes for food change. It takes more to feed them. Hopefully and finally, we look forward to the day when they are not only doing these things on their own, but beginning these steps with the next generation. When they do, it is important for us to remind them that babies do not mature into adults overnight.

Spiritual development is not much different from physical development. New Christians constantly need the basics; it is not healthy for them to develop too quickly or for them to stop growing before the work has been completed. If you are wondering when that work will be done, the answer is, "you are not there yet."

How do we approach this new life? At the outset, it is important to realize that we are used to living in darkness (Rom. 1:21–23). We are used to living for ourselves (John 21:18). We are even used to following our own passions (Eph. 2:1–3). For these reasons, a different walk must be developed (Eph. 4:20)—and as toddlers, we are going to stumble as we begin to walk anew (Heb. 4:15–16).

What are the things newborn babes need? They need the foundational realities upon which all Scripture is built. I caution you: Do not take for granted the simple truths of Scripture. In Matthew 22:34–40, Jesus is approached with a highly theological question. How does He answer? He answers with spiritual milk and finishes with meat. Sometimes we think too little about the basic tenets of the Christian faith and only want to talk about the difficult things. Jesus has proven to us that the simple things are critical to our understanding and our ability to take on the more difficult things of faith with humility.

There is a phenomenon among college students that is very interesting to me. I have in jest called this "sophmoritis" (not a real word, of course), because seemingly every college sophomore comes home from that second year believing all the adults around them are intellectually challenged. I have to admit that after my second year of biblical training, I sat down with my father, who had been pastoring for 28 years at the time, and instructed him on all of the things he was doing wrong and needed to change at his church. In short, sophmoritis is the inclination to believe, after acquiring a little bit of knowledge, that we have become experts.

It is very easy to think that because we have begun a journey with Christ that includes some of the heavier issues of Scripture, our opinions about these matters should carry weight. I believe that grappling with these weighty issues is necessary in the life of believers and part of their growth, but such issues must be approached carefully and humbly. Scripture has the most significant impact in the lives of the humble (Jas. 4:6).

Simple theology is important because it is sustainable for every believer. It provides sure, foundational truth that is easily remembered and creates strong believers who are ready for any circumstance (Eph. 4:14–16).

There is an important balance to be achieved here. Milk will not provide continued growth. Eventually growing believers will have to take on more difficult things, or they will be limited in their ability to strengthen others. This is no different from an athlete who does not push himself once he has met a certain goal. Athletes know that goals are not the end of the line: they are just steps on a journey. They are always pushing themselves to run faster, jump farther, throw more accurately. That is the mindset needed for a child of God. A little bit of Jesus is necessary, but more of Him is always better.

While we are growing—which is pretty much always—there will be times of difficulty in which we need something other than high-level "strength" training. I remember a time when I experienced conflict with other believers that resulted in my needing to swallow my pride and take the beating for the sake of others. During that time, I experienced great and tiring doubt about the church and the gospel. I began to wonder for the first time since I had been renewed in Christ Jesus whether this whole Christian thing was really worth it. I could not find the strength to study. I could not motivate myself to pray or write. After several days of spiritual starvation, I came across a simple little devotional book by Charles Swindoll entitled "Perfect Trust." I began to read this small book one chapter at a time and the spiritual milk began to renew me with sustenance. Eventually I was able to take on more difficult theological things again. But this spiritual milk in a time of great weakness is what the Lord knew I needed to get back on my feet. Since that time (more than a decade ago), I spend some time with Swindoll's little book every year.

Spiritual milk is for everyone who has believed the gospel of Christ, for everyone who is experiencing its transforming power. Let's not forget to find nourishment in the simple truths.

? ≡   Responding to God's Word in our lives:

- In what way are you living in pursuit of the nourishing Word of God?

- How are the stories shaping you?

- How are the letters affecting your thinking?

- If you expect to grow in your relationship with Jesus, you need to begin a regular diet of nourishing spiritual food.

- Determine a good time for regular Bible study and reading.

- Determine a method for accountability.

- Find a person whom you can connect with to discuss what God is teaching you.

7

Resting in Zion

1 Peter 2:4–8:

As you come to him, a living stone rejected by men but in the sight of God chosen and precious, (5) you yourselves like living stones are being built up as a spiritual house, to be a holy priesthood, to offer spiritual sacrifices acceptable to God through Jesus Christ. (6) For it stands in Scripture: "Behold, I am laying in Zion a stone, a cornerstone chosen and precious, and whoever believes in him will not be put to shame." (7) So the honor is for you who believe, but for those who do not believe, the stone that the builders rejected has become the cornerstone, (8) and a stone of stumbling, and a rock of offense. They stumble because they disobey the word, as they were destined to do.

"Come Just as You Are" is a famous song used by the beloved evangelist Billy Graham on countless occasions to invite people to come to Jesus for salvation. When we come to Him, we come bringing our burdens, desperately hopeless and without a home. We come to Jesus knowing that He is different from those things we have turned to in the past.

Jesus is not an idol made by man. He was not created, but rather was the creator of life (John 1:1–3). He is the one who looks into darkness and overcomes it (John 1:3–4). The Bible also states that He is the stone who will crush the kingdoms set up by men (Dan. 2:34). He is the one and only living God (Acts 17:29).

Despite all of this, He was regarded as unworthy by Israel because He was not what they had expected or determined He would be, and therefore was not what they wanted — even though He was the one they needed. While the world rejected Him, the Father was delighting in His Son (Mark 1:9–10).

Jesus knows our burdens, our hopelessness, our desperate desire to be different than we have been (Heb. 4:14–15). Because He is one who has experienced our pain, we can surrender to Him. We follow the Lord who has been rejected by those He loves. We learn from the Savior who does what is right/obedient/good when everyone is shouting, "you are wrong." We lean on the man who would not give up because His purpose was too important. He has already demonstrated His power as servant. We are watching, hoping, and remaining steadfast until He displays His power as King when He returns.

We are not becoming gods, as some would have us believe. But we are becoming a better reflection of Christ. We will never "be" Jesus, but we can display similarities to Him because of our relationship to Him and the power He has provided to us through the Holy Spirit.

We are being shaped into His likeness by a process that will be fulfilled by Jesus who cannot fail in delivering on His promise. He is molding us into individuals who can glorify God through their labors, and thus we are becoming more effective ministers of God. And together, we are being formed into the church.

This message is not new; it was firmly planted in Scripture. We put our faith in Jesus because He is our sure foundation. Our every expectation will be satisfied in Him.

So, what can be expected? Those in Christ will find immediate restoration of the soul into right relationship with God. They become an established part of the church, with a specialized purpose, in the church of God. They will also find themselves positioned as holy priests, offering sacrifices acceptable to God.

Those who reject Jesus Christ have rejected the foundation stone without which humanity cannot find restoration. They are offended by His message, thinking "who is He to say we need a Savior?" Those same people will continue to fall short of God's requirement for salvation because they will not turn to Him, and therefore they are destined to live in disobedience.

?≡ Responding to God's Word in our lives:

I know we have gone over this often, but it is foundational to everything else.

- Have you believed on Jesus Christ for salvation?

- If you have not, then what are you waiting for?

If you have trusted in Jesus for your salvation, then are you living to become more like Him?

- How are you spending time in His Word?

- How are you obeying what it says?

- How are you prayerfully trusting Jesus to do what is right and good with your life?

- What steps can you take to put all of your hope in what Jesus is going to do with your life and the eternity He has prepared for you?

This is not a process that you should be undertaking solo.

- Find a local church family that teaches the Word of God.

- Invest in relationships with other believers who are seeking to grow in their faith also.

8

Setting an Example of Godly Living

1 Peter 2:9–3:12:

But you are a chosen race, a royal priesthood, a holy nation, a people for his own possession, that you may proclaim the excellencies of him who called you out of darkness into his marvelous light. (10) Once you were not a people, but now you are God's people; once you had not received mercy, but now you have received mercy. (11) Beloved, I urge you as sojourners and exiles to abstain from the passions of the flesh, which wage war against your soul. (12) Keep your conduct among the Gentiles honorable, so that when they speak against you as evildoers, they may see your good deeds and glorify God on the day of visitation. (13) Be subject for the Lord's sake to every human institution, whether it be to the emperor as supreme, (14) or to governors as sent by him to punish those who do evil and to praise those who do good. (15) For this is the will of God, that by doing good you should put to silence the ignorance of foolish people. (16) Live as people who are free, not using your freedom as a cover-up for evil, but living as servants of God. (17) Honor everyone. Love the brotherhood. Fear God. Honor the emperor. (18) Servants, be subject to your masters with all respect, not only to the good and gentle but also to the unjust. (19) For this is a gracious thing, when, mindful of God, one endures sorrows while suffering unjustly. (20) For what credit is it if, when you sin and are beaten for it, you endure? But if when you do good and suffer for it you endure, this is a gracious thing in the sight of God. (21) For to this you have been called, because Christ also suffered for you, leaving you an example, so that you might follow in his steps. (22) He committed no sin, neither was deceit found in his mouth. (23) When he was reviled, he did not revile in return; when he suffered, he did not threaten, but continued entrusting himself to him who judges justly. (24) He himself bore our sins in his body on the tree, that we might die to sin and live to righteousness. By his wounds you have been healed. (25) For you were straying like sheep, but have now returned to the Shepherd and Overseer of your souls.

(3:1) Likewise, wives, be subject to your own husbands, so that even if some do not obey the word, they may be won without a word by the conduct of their wives, (2) when they see your respectful and pure conduct. (3) Do not let your adorning be external—the braiding of hair and the putting on of gold jewelry, or the clothing you wear— (4) but let your adorning be the hidden person of the heart with the imperishable beauty of a gentle and quiet spirit, which in God's sight is very precious. (5) For this is how the holy women who hoped in God used to adorn themselves, by submitting to their own husbands, (6) as Sarah obeyed Abraham, calling him lord. And you are her children, if you do good and do not fear anything that is frightening. (7) Likewise, husbands, live with your wives in an understanding way, showing honor to the woman as the weaker vessel, since they are heirs with you of the grace of life, so that your prayers may not be hindered. (8) Finally, all of you, have unity of mind, sympathy, brotherly love, a tender heart, and a humble mind. (9) Do not repay evil for evil or reviling for reviling, but on the contrary, bless, for to this you were called, that you may obtain a blessing. (10) For whoever desires to love life and see good days, let him keep his tongue from evil and his lips from speaking deceit; (11) let him turn away from evil and do good; let him seek peace and pursue it. (12) For the eyes of the Lord are on the righteous, and his ears are open to their prayer. But the face of the Lord is against those who do evil.

The singular purpose of Christian living is to glorify God. The proclamation of Christ through every opportunity, means, or engagement we have, both in our speech and in our example, is one of the most wonderful ways we are privileged to do so. We have been chosen by God to minister in this world and to represent Him in our dealings — in other words, to be His people. We have the opportunity to verbally acknowledge our dependent surrender to Him and to testify to the change He has brought to our lives. We were blind and now we see. We were once desperately seeking forgiveness but now we have been forgiven. We were once alone and now we are part of a family.

We have been freed from our debt and left with a question of response. How will we respond to the one who has saved our souls? Will we live for ourselves, or will we live devoted to the one who has saved us?

Practical Christian living consists of placing the flesh under submission to Christ rather than living to indulge its desires. We have not been freed from the penalty of sin so that we may continue in it. Instead, we have been given the ability to fight against the desires within us that bring destruction to our lives. We have been empowered to live beyond daily satisfaction and unto daily honor.

In fact, we have the opportunity to stand out, in the eyes of unbelievers, as those who are different. We do not live as snobs who cannot go out among the unclean, nor as separatists engaged in their own little closed-off society. Instead, we go about as those who are living in this world changed, different, causing wonder about what has happened to us.

The followers of Christ will live in submission to the government as the established authority in their lives ordained by God. As followers of Christ, we do not have the freedom to dishonor the government over us nor the luxury of mocking the president. We do not have to agree with him or promote him, but we do have to show him honor. For the sake of the gospel we separate our political dissatisfaction from our response to the office that individual holds. We do not do this out of service to the officeholder, but out of service to God.

It is a great responsibility for followers of Christ to show honor to their superiors in the workplace even when those superiors do not deserve it. Rarely do we meet individuals whose bosses think of the employee first and themselves as servants. You probably do not agree with every decision your boss makes. You may even work for someone of morally questionable or even downright terrible character. If such persons are your superiors, you must still treat them with respect. Suffering under the authority of unjust persons for their good conforms you to the image of Christ.

Women who are living in submission to God live as though the way they live toward their husbands daily is of utmost importance. Here is the big question: Is the God of the Universe powerful enough to lead a wife where He desires for her to be through the decisions of her naturally imperfect spouse? Christian wives do not live in submission to their husbands because they fully trust those men. Christian wives live in submission to their husbands because those husbands are not powerful enough to ruin God's plan for their lives. By submitting to their husbands in obedience to God, they are submitting not just to their husbands but to God.

Christian wives do this: live in submission to their husbands, hoping that their husbands will follow their example and in turn submit to God. A Christian wife's desire is to be a wife who establishes in her home a selfless obedience to God. A Christian wife makes her husband love the woman he lives with rather than enticing him through her appearance, knowing that outward beauty will not last and the inward beauty of a loving wife will continue to grow throughout the marriage.

Men who are living for God carry the weight of life in their homes. Women are not lesser beings. They are made in the image of God just as men are. They are intelligent, organized, and often more observant than men are.

As a result, most wives are overburdened with keeping up the home and the family. Some respond to this by determining that "this is just the way life is" or by finding identity in the perfection of their homes. Some fantasize about the life they dreamed of before marriage. Because of this, most wives are not drawn to their husbands as a leader and friend, but instead think of them as just another person to care for who happens to bring home a paycheck.

Remember this, guys: Before God, it is not mama's house. He holds you responsible for what your home is like. Your wife is there to join you in the work. She is not there to do the work for you. If the world is going to determine that Christ in our lives makes us different from other men, we must be the husbands God has instructed us to be.

Within the body of Christ, we purposefully seek to live peacefully despite our sinful actions. Forgiveness means saying "I forgive you." This reality must establish us as different from the rest of the world. If the body of Christ is living a life of forgiveness and its individuals are living lives of forgiveness, then the world will believe there is hope for us in Christ.

When an individual's life is dedicated to honoring God; that individual will live in God's favor. A lack of self-imposed hardship is removed from the life of an individual who follows Christ, and a lack of drama accompanies the individual who does not need to talk all the time. A better life will come to those who are not looking for a fight. But even greater than all these things is this: If our lives are difficult despite our efforts to do good, it is because the reproach we carry is the result of living for Jesus.

If we are following Him in obedience, we will one day stand before Him faithful. That is our goal. That is our desire. That is our pursuit. We want one day to stand before the Lord and be found faithful.

Some are facing difficult work situations. Some are facing difficult marriages. Some are facing a fearful time of government leadership. In whatever situation you find yourself today, it is important to do these things:

- Obey Jesus at His Word.

- Surrender to His authority.

- Allow Him to do His healing work in your life.

- Let His grace be what keeps you strong.

- Trust Him when it seems you cannot trust anyone else.

?≡ Responding to God's Word in our lives:

Probably one of the most significant problems in Christianity is our unwillingness to obey the Bible in a practical way. This chapter is an introduction to the practical applications of 1 Peter. Would you commit to:

- Making a self-assessment about the things studied in the upcoming chapters?

- Confessing sin as to where you are not living obediently as you study these chapters?

- Obeying the Holy Spirit's instruction not just in your words but also in your actions?

9

So Much More than Heaven Bound!

1 Peter 2:9–10:
But you are a chosen race, a royal priesthood, a holy nation, a people for his own possession, that you may proclaim the excellencies of him who called you out of darkness into his marvelous light. (10) Once you were not a people, but now you are God's people; once you had not received mercy, but now you have received mercy.

As evangelists sharing the gospel of Christ, I think we often miss the whole point when we begin our approach by saying, "Do you want to spend an eternity in heaven?" Of course the answer is yes, if the question is being met with the truth in an individual's heart and not some kind of sarcasm. Nobody wants to spend eternity in torment and suffering. Most would not want to spend eternity in the fallen world we have now. The real question is whether or not they realize that sin has separated them from the creator of all things and that this world has been ruined as a result of our inability to yield ourselves to His authority. If they realize and understand this, then — when Jesus' death and resurrection are presented as the means of establishing that relationship once again and placing humankind under the rule of a just and right ruler — they would come to Jesus better understanding what it is they have given themselves to.

It will come as no surprise that the singular purpose of Christian living is the proclamation of Christ through every opportunity, means, or engagement we have, both in our speech and in our example. In contrast, those who have rejected Christ are by nature disobedient (1 Peter 2:8).

We are a chosen race. We were pulled out of our old sin-pursuing, lust-indulgent, rebellious lives. This saving, done by the election of God unto His redeeming work in us, is done because God sought to do this in and through us. He overcame the things that were keeping us from Him. He overcame our rejection of His perfect plan for our lives (Rom. 3:10–11). He showed us the tragic end of living life according to our own terms (Ps. 14:1–3). He opened our eyes to the dangerous, terrible realities of our own sin life, making clear to us the darkness that dwells within (Ps 52:1–3). When we realize our salvation is not the result of anything we have done, we must admit that, at the very least, this election means we were not left hopeless to deal with our own depravity. Without the intervention of the Holy Spirit, we would not have chosen God.

We have become related to Christ. When we die with Christ and are risen with Christ, we have been given a transfusion of blood. We once were children of Adam but are now children of God. As His children, we take His name and live according to His ways. Our names have been added to the Father's final will and testament, making us inheritors of all that is His.

God has chosen to make us part of His family and given us all the rights that pertain to naturally born children (Eph. 1:11–14). That choice has not been made because of our significance as individuals. It was made because of our need to be rescued from our own sinfulness and to have our sin debt paid. We were hopelessly lost, and God through Christ Jesus provided us salvation, a family, and a future.

We have been strategically positioned in this world as God's messengers. Consider this:

Royals = Those who establish rule.

Priesthood = Those called to perform religious rites and duties on behalf of others.

We are the only hope our world has for understanding God's plans and purposes. If we do not stand up for truth, the world around us will be left to its own natural instincts. But there is a warning: We do not establish God's rule according to our own desires. We are representatives of His desires and we do not instruct according to our own opinions. We are bound by the teachings of Scripture.

How, then, do we establish God's ways in this world if we do not know His ways? We cannot afford to be ignorant of God's instruction for our lives and we cannot afford to be content with little knowledge of the Holy One. Our calling in this world as believers requires our pursuit of biblical understanding. We study the Word and obey what we learn. Then we teach those around us how to do the same.

Where we are, and those with whom we have been put in contact, are not coincidences. These things are ordained by God. We are the light given to the life of those around us, and we may be the light which leads to their salvation. Unfortunately, we may be the light which leaves them without excuse for their rejection. But our role is to shine in their lives in hopes that they will see our Savior and desire Him (Matt. 5:14–16).

The church of Jesus Christ is a nation of people set apart from the rest of the world, whose god is the devil. We are not a nation of people who live within physical boundaries. Rather, we are a nation of people who live according to a higher calling. For this reason, our submission to what is legal according to law is too simplistic. Our submission goes beyond what is legal and seeks the good of others (Gal. 5:13–14). We are a nation of people who live our daily lives morally accountable to God for our actions rather than just the accountability of men (Jas. 4:17).

We are not our own. We were bought back from sin through the shed blood of Jesus Christ to live for Him (1 Cor. 6:19–20). When we were redeemed by the blood of Christ, we turned away from a life of self to a life of surrender to Jesus (Matt. 16:24).

We were made into a race, nation, people whose sole purpose in this world is the proclamation of Jesus Christ. We proclaim the reality of our fallenness and our inability to understand or do what is right before God. We proclaim the power of Christ to make us into the individuals we could not be on our own. We do not proclaim something we do not know but rather the transformation that has taken place in us through Jesus.

We live in praise of the one (Jesus) who changed everything. We were living life according to our own perspective without accountability, direction, or help. We were hopelessly seeking forgiveness for the things we had done in ignorance to destroy ourselves and others. Now we belong to a family whose identity and pursuits align with eternal purpose and we have found forgiveness and hope in the one (Jesus) who cannot fail.

If you belong to Jesus, then you have been transformed by Him and every day you live is an opportunity to share that with the people you come into contact with. Don't take this role for granted. Don't forget the purpose you have here on earth. And don't live in fear of those who will reject what Jesus has done for them on the cross. Continually share Christ and live for Christ. Continually invite those around you to learn of Him. Celebrate the opportunity to do what God has called each of us to do.

?≡ Responding to God's Word in our lives:

- Would you think through these things today?

- If you are still living life apart from Jesus, then come join the family.

  - Admit to God that you are a sinner.

  - Acknowledge that your sin qualifies you for judgment in hell.

  - Ask God to forgive your sin based on the death Jesus endured for you on the cross.

  - Surrender to Jesus as the only means of salvation from death and living a life that will bring glory to God.

  - Turn from living in disobedience to God and walk with Jesus in the new life provided by His resurrection from the dead.

- If you are an individual transformed by the power of Jesus Christ, then make sure you are on track with His purposes in this world.

  - Name some areas where you have been unwilling to be conformed to His ways.

  - What plans of yours can be put aside to further Jesus' plans instead?

  - Make a specific determination to follow His leading in your life, whatever that may be.

  - Write out how you will trust His Word to guide you in your decision making.

10

Gospel-Driven Sacrifice

1 Peter 2:11–12:
Beloved, I urge you as sojourners and exiles to abstain from the passions of the flesh, which wage war against your soul. (12) Keep your conduct among the Gentiles honorable, so that when they speak against you as evildoers, they may see your good deeds and glorify God on the day of visitation.

Practical Christian living is found in placing the flesh under submission to Christ rather than living to indulge its desires. Our calling, as seen in 2 Peter 9–10, is the proclamation of the gospel. Our future will be culminated at the return of Christ. At that point our pursuits in this world will be weighed and our eternal rewards will be clearly seen (1 Cor. 3:10–14). Even though we know this, we often get caught up in worrying about today rather than the future.

There are many things we choose to worry about. Some are concerned about wasting the time we have. Others are worried about completing a "bucket list." Many are afraid of missing out on something great life has to offer. So, life is pursued passionately, energetically, and indulgently. We do this even though we know that a life that looks only at the temporal, even if well lived, has been lived in vain.

Solomon, King of Israel, ends Ecclesiastes 2 this way: *There is nothing better for a person than that he should eat and drink and find enjoyment in his toil. This also, I saw, is from the hand of God, (25) for apart from him who can eat or who can have enjoyment? (26) For to the one who pleases him God has given wisdom and knowledge and joy, but to the sinner he has given the business of gathering and collecting, only to give to one who pleases God. This also is vanity and a striving after the wind.*

It is important to keep some things in mind. The temporal things are vanity. Everything will be given to those who please God. Remember, we are here for the sake of the gospel.

Can I ask of you what Peter has asked? While we live in this world, which is opposed to God and unwilling to acknowledge the realities of their sin, do not give in to the things that will lead you away from your relationship with Christ.

What are these desires of the flesh (Gal. 5:19–21)? There are many, so this list is not exhaustive. Rather, it is something to think about as you examine your life. If there are other things that draw you away from Christ, then include those also in your reflection.

- The desire to have sex with whomever we want whenever we want.

- Taking what is good and using it for evil.

- Living for the satisfaction of sensual desires.

- The worship of created things rather than the creator.

- The use of drugs or sorcery to satisfy a curiosity or longing.

- The creating of lines; having enemies.

- Conflicts resulting from personality differences or competing desires.

- The rage that comes when someone has what you want.

- Reaction based in a dissatisfaction with life or a situation.

- A feeling that arises when someone is standing between you and something you want.

- When a group is broken into two opposing groups.

- An ill will toward someone who has something you cannot have.

- Consuming more alcohol than the body can handle without losing control.

- Unrestrained indulgences, often influenced by alcohol or drugs.

So, how do we keep from fulfilling the desires of the flesh (Rom. 8:5–8)? One way is to stop devoting mental space to your desires.

A proactive measure is to invest mental energy in the things of the Spirit. What are the things we should be devoting our minds to (Phil. 4:8)? First and foremost, devote yourself to knowing and understanding the truth (John 17:17). Gain an understanding of justice in love and grace, and in doing so learn how to show honor to those who should receive honor. Discipline yourself to enjoy what God has created for us without sin. Admire what is good and talk about things that strengthen, encourage, and edify. Godliness is not automatic. It is practiced (1 Tim. 4:7–8).

We find further instruction in James 1:26–27. We do not tell the unbelievers of this world how to act. Instead, we show them a different way. We help those who are going through difficult circumstances and take care in the way we communicate with those around us. It is also important to be conscious about the things to which we devote our time.

Why do we devote ourselves to living the way Christ has asked us to live? The believer's desire is to live in such a way that even if those with whom they are sharing Christ will not accept the message, they will not be able to condemn it, because of its outworking and evidence in our lives. For believers who have lived well, when accusations come against them — and they will — the accusations will not stick because of the lives they have lived (John 19:1–4).

The goal of this life is not the gratification of temporal desires or the accumulation of temporal gains. The physical things of this world which will not be carried into eternity are good things given to us by a good God and they are to be used for His purposes. Things in and of themselves are not bad. Possessions and accomplishments are not in themselves evil. Instead of casting them aside, we use them with the understanding that they are a means to accomplish the task before us rather than the goal of our lives. We enjoy those things God has created for us in this world and we find satisfaction in Christ and participation in the work He has called us to.

The goal of this life is the reward that will one day be made manifest by Christ. This goal cannot be accomplished through the lives of individuals determined to live for the satisfaction of self. Rather, it is accomplished in the lives of those who are surrendered to the cause of Christ, which is the proclamation of the gospel to a lost and dying world (2 Tim. 2:1–3).

?≡ Responding to God's Word in our lives:

- Are you living for yourself and according to your own ways or design for life, or are you surrendered to God's ways and design for the life of all those who claim to be under His care?

- If you are living surrendered to God's ways and design for your life, how is that demonstrated in your life in a practical way?

- Are there still areas where you are living for your own purposes? Name them and lay out a path for taking their control away.

- As you look at the things in this chapter which hinder us from living out Christ in our lives, determine to request Jesus' forgiveness for these things, surrender to the pursuit of life according to Jesus' direction, and follow through with what you have seen is the way of Christ Jesus in His Word, trusting in His power through the Holy Spirit to accomplish His desire in you.

11

Submission to Those Who Rule Proves Our Faith in God

1 Peter 2:13–17:

Be subject for the Lord's sake to every human institution, whether it be to the emperor as supreme, (14) or to governors as sent by him to punish those who do evil and to praise those who do good. (15) For this is the will of God, that by doing good you should put to silence the ignorance of foolish people. (16) Live as people who are free, not using your freedom as a cover-up for evil, but living as servants of God. (17) Honor everyone. Love the brotherhood. Fear God. Honor the emperor.

In a former time, I was a pretty good high school athlete. At five feet seven and one-half inches tall and 130 pounds, I was never really going to do much more than that. During those years I engaged with more than one coach who insisted on a way of doing things that I did not agree with. Often my sinful attitude would get the best of me and I would go my own way. *"There is a way that seems right unto man but the ways thereof are the ways of death."* I wish I had known this verse back then; it would have saved me from a lot of splinters. (For nonathletes, that means I didn't get to play, and instead warmed the bench.)

I know that obedience to authority is difficult, especially when we do not agree with those authorities. What I am hoping to show here is that submission to authority is not submission to an individual. It is submission to God through submission to His established authority in our lives.

Why do we have individuals who rule over us? First of all, rulers are the result of mankind's unwillingness to submit to God. We have rulers to rule over us so that we are not each left to decide for ourselves between right and wrong (Judg. 21:25). Rulers bring order in a fallen world by determining what is best for society and protecting the weak from the strong.

Unfortunately, having human kings and rulers brings with it some difficult realities. Israel was given a warning when they asked for a king to rule over them instead of God (1 Sam. 8:1–18). Rulers will take your sons and use them for their purposes (8:12). Rulers will take your daughters and use them for their purposes (8:13). Rulers will require a portion of your earnings (taxes) (8:14–17). The rulers chosen by us will not be or do what we thought, but they will be the ones we have chosen (8:18).

We must be realistic about the results of having rulers. Do not let those who are influential—whether good or bad—scare us into thinking the next leader will make or break our country. "We won't ever recover from it!" a well-known church leader said; "we will go down in flames, maybe literally, if we put the wrong person in power." Statements like these remove our faith from God and put it in the hands of mortal man.

From 1050 BC to 930 BC, Israel had three kings. Saul was quite literally crazy. David was a man after God's own heart except in his dealing with Uriah the Hittite and his union with Uriah's wife. Then there was Solomon: some interesting things happened under Solomon's rule. Taxes were higher than at any time in history to support his agenda and the country grew to its largest point in history. He took 700 wives and 300 concubines and began worshiping the false gods of his wives. After his death, Solomon's idolatry would be the reason for a national split.

Since the time of Solomon, Israel has experienced many hardships and tragedies. The country was split into two—Israel to the south and Judah to the north. They were in captivity under Egypt and returned to a broken land. They lived under imperialism. They suffered the loss of land to Palestine, though control over a portion of what was promised was restored to them by God.

Christianity has survived despite the rule of many wicked kings and emperors. It even survived under the heresy of the Catholic church. War broke out as Protestants separated from Catholics. In addition, the Catholic church had its own internal rifts and conflicts to overcome.

So, it is important to understand that rulers are not going to do—cannot do—what we expect them to do. God has maintained the care of his people through every age. Why does the church survive? The church survives because God is in control.

Only those who are living in submission to God can submit to human government without fear. Because we believe God is in control, we can surrender to the human rulers who have been placed over us. As laws are enacted, we follow them to the extent they do not go against what God has instructed. For example, Daniel submissively rejected the king's food. He even continued to pray daily when it became illegal to do so. Shadrach, Meshach, and Abednego refused to bow to the king's idol. The apostles refused to stop preaching the name of Jesus Christ and were willing to take the punishment for it.

We submit to the authority of human rulers because submission to them is submission to the will of God. For example, we submit to police officers, judges, and tax collectors. It is their job to maintain order amid those who do not want any authority in their lives at all. It is their job to protect those who live in obedience to the law. Our submission to authority silences those who would call us troublemakers. We show that we are seeking what is best for our world and not trying to start a revolution.

But we stand firm on the foundation, which is Jesus Christ, and on that foundation we will not be moved. If our convictions are at odds with the ruling authority, then we stand fast and take the punishment for doing maintaining our beliefs. We do not revolt against them. If our convictions result in our imprisonment, then we will be the best prisoners they have ever seen.

When we are living in submission to Christ by obeying the authority of those who rule over us, we show our freedom to the world. We give honor to the ruler as one who has been given authority by God. We do not use freedom, which is an ability to do right, as an opportunity to do wrong. We use the reality of our position before Christ to serve Him through our submission to ruling authority. We realize the importance of showing temporal authorities the honor they deserve as image bearers. We trust that the God of the universe, who establishes and tears down kingdoms at His will, is in control of what is taking place.

?≡   Responding to God's Word in our lives:

- Who are the authorities in your life?

- In what ways have you been opposing those authorities rather than submitting to them?

- Do you need to repent of your actions?

- Do you need to seek their forgiveness?

- How can you bring honor to Christ in your submission to authorities going forward?

12

The Faithful Servant Entrusts Himself to God's Care

1 Peter 2:18–24:

Servants, be subject to your masters with all respect, not only to the good and gentle but also to the unjust. (19) For this is a gracious thing, when, mindful of God, one endures sorrows while suffering unjustly. (20) For what credit is it if, when you sin and are beaten for it, you endure? But if when you do good and suffer for it you endure, this is a gracious thing in the sight of God. (21) For to this you have been called, because Christ also suffered for you, leaving you an example, so that you might follow in his steps. (22) He committed no sin, neither was deceit found in his mouth. (23) When he was reviled, he did not revile in return; when he suffered, he did not threaten, but continued entrusting himself to him who judges justly. (24) He himself bore our sins in his body on the tree, that we might die to sin and live to righteousness. For you were straying like sheep, but have now returned to the shepherd and Overseer of your souls.

Have you ever had a bad boss? Those individuals with authority over you who seem to be on a power trip or more concerned about their own benefit than the welfare of those around them. Maybe they make it hard for you to get a promotion or a raise. You might even know that you have a better understanding of the job than they do, but for some reason they have been given authority over you. Of course, this is not unusual. In reality, the opposite situation is the rare one: The situation where the bosses are more concerned about those under their employment than with themselves. The situation where the authority/boss is a great leader whom everyone is eager to follow.

Because the difficult boss/authority/employer is more common than the good one, it is crucial for our testimony and encouragement that we understand our role in this difficult place. It is crucial for us to remember that even in these situations God has not left us alone or lost control.

When we are living under the authority of other human beings, we faithfully obey them, with a desire to honor their rule over us. By serving those in authority over us, both publicly and in secret, we seek to please Christ through our diligent care of them (Eph. 6:5–8). We obey employers because they determine our livelihood; this means that we are not two-faced, kissing up to them when they are around and speaking badly of them when they are not around. From a pure heart, we seek to honor God through service to them and we serve them knowing that in serving them well God will reward us.

We serve our employers by obediently doing our jobs without argument and honestly using their supplies and resources (Tit. 2:9–10). We do good work for our employers. We resist the desire to argue with our employers about the work given to us and how it should be done. We do not take for ourselves supplies or other things that belong to our employers. We make ourselves trustworthy in use of the equipment and supplies we have been given. Our obedience and trustworthiness present Christ as a real and powerful part of our lives.

We do not honor our employers because they are worthy, we honor them out of obedience to Christ. When our obedience in service to authorities is driven by a love for Christ, the stature of our authorities carries little weight. If they are good masters, then we are blessed by that and seek to be a blessing to them. If they are difficult to serve, we serve with honor despite their ungrateful attitude toward us.

When we faithfully and obediently serve those in authority over us, whatever their attitude toward us, we find favor with God. This favor comes through a desire to serve Him by serving our authorities and through the enduring devotion we show to our authorities when mistreated by them. It also comes to us while we are facing difficult circumstances at the hands of our authorities and still treating them with respect.

Conversely, we do not gain favor from God when we do not fulfill our responsibilities to the authorities we have been given and face punishment for it. Certainly, there is no favor when we continue in the work we have been given while disrespecting, acting dishonestly toward, or disobeying the authorities we have been given because we do not think they are worthy.

There is a better way to live. We live in obedience to God through our service to our authorities. We willingly suffer despite our obedience. We do not give up doing good to and for them. It is through these actions that God's favor will come upon us.

Why do we gain God's favor when we suffer while doing good to those who cause our suffering? It is because His favor accrues to those who are fulfilling the calling of Christlikeness and we are following the example that we have been given (Rom. 5:6–8).

We are never a greater reflection of Christ than when we show love to an individual who may never show that love back to us. Christ is the example for those who suffer unjustly. In His life lived here on earth, Jesus never did anything wrong, never lied or manipulated situations to His advantage; even though He was struck down physically, mentally, and emotionally. He never abused those who were abusing Him. He endured suffering while doing good, trusting God to deal with the outcome of His obedience.

He willingly served us to the point of death on a cross. The shedding of His blood gives us the means to die to sin and His resurrection gives us the power to live for Him, in Him, and through Him. He restored us through His obedience because He realized our hopelessness apart from His work in our lives.

We endure suffering as servants of Christ so that we may serve those who cause our suffering in a desire to see them come to Christ. We work well under the care of good employers in a desire to see them come to Christ. We serve them, trusting them into God's care and trusting that as we do this we will live in His favor, which is worth more than any reward, satisfaction, or physical pleasure this world can offer.

We must see that our way is found in Christ's example and our power is found in Christ's work. His purpose is our purpose. He realized our lostness and came into the world to save us through the cross. He calls us to follow Him home. Then, once we are home, He calls us to go out and lead others to Him.

Do not be confused by wrong thinking. Your work is not your work. It is a means provided by Christ for the furtherance of the gospel.

?≡   Responding to God's Word in our lives:

- Is it enough for you that through your dedicated service to your employer Jesus will be glorified?

- How are you serving your employer well for the sake of the gospel?

- Are there areas in which you need to repent of your attitude or actions toward your employer because they did not glorify Jesus?

13

Living Well in Marriage

1 Peter 3:1–7:

Likewise, wives, be subject to your own husbands, so that even if some do not obey the word, they may be won without a word by the conduct of their wives, (2) when they see your respectful and pure conduct. (3) Do not let your adorning be external—the braiding of hair and the putting on of gold jewelry, or the clothing you wear— (4) but let your adorning be the hidden person of the heart with the imperishable beauty of a gentle and quiet spirit, which in God's sight is very precious. (5) For this is how the holy women who hoped in God used to adorn themselves, by submitting to their own husbands, (6) as Sarah obeyed Abraham, calling him lord. And you are her children, if you do good and do not fear anything that is frightening.

(7) Likewise, husbands, live with your wives in an understanding way, showing honor to the woman as the weaker vessel, since they are heirs with you of the grace of life, so that your prayers may not be hindered.

Marriage relationships are not easy. They are full of ups and downs. Primary among the conditions of marriage is vulnerability to an individual whom we hope loves us enough to deal with our imperfections—imperfections that we may have been able to hide from everyone else. We deal with changes to our physical appearance throughout the relationship. Life, experience, struggle, pain, joy, and suffering all begin to show themselves in us physically, emotionally, and spiritually.

While in this life-altering relationship, which we have committed to till death, there are things we must figure out about one another. There are things we must learn about how this relationship will function. There are also things that do not have to be figured out. In this portion of Scripture, Peter describes how to be married in obedience to God and His ways for marriage which will make the marriage work the way it should even in the most difficult of situations.

A woman who is in a marital relationship with a man should be submissive to the man she has married (Luke 2:51). Therefore, be cautious in pursuing marriage. Women are not subject to men they do not marry, so they should choose wisely whom they will marry. She must determine that her husband's obedience to God is not a prerequisite to her submission in the relationship; her submission is to the Word of God rather than her husband's expectations.

A Christian woman submits to her husband in a desire to see him become obedient to God—not because she nagged him to do it! Instead, through submission in marriage she demonstrates to him what submission looks like (Luke 9:22–24). Submission in marriage is not any different than the submission demonstrated when Jesus went to the cross. Jesus submitted to our need by putting our good before His own. Jesus suffered so that we would be changed. In marriage (especially difficult marriages), an individual's personal "happiness" is put aside for the good of the spouse, in the hope that this will cause the spouse to see Christ. Husbands can be won over to Christ by wives who demonstrate submission.

Do not allow your external beauty to be the basis of your significance, whether to self, mankind, or God. Be more than physically beautiful and do not delight in your natural beauty. Do not flaunt your looks, intelligence, or status as something that makes you superior. Instead, make the greatest part of you be who you are inside. Grow in areas that will not decline with age (1 Tim. 4:7b–8). Seek to find glory in what God sees. Whether in marriage or any other position, relationship, or responsibility that you carry, it is vitally important for you, as a follower of Jesus, to place total significance in how God will interpret your decisions. The first, next, and final question regarding every action is: Will He be glorified or disappointed by what you have done?

An honorable goal is to become like the women of faith. They made themselves obedient to their husbands and embraced their husbands as heads of the home. We are the result of their obedience to God's plan for the home. They have demonstrated what can take place when we trust God even though we are afraid of what may happen.

To a man who has taken a woman to be his wife: Learn everything you can about the woman with whom you are living this life. Know her physical needs, desires, and limits. Know her emotional strengths and struggles, including her dreams. Just as you learned everything you could in a desire to win her heart, spend the rest of your days learning how to love her more completely.

Decide that she is an individual who deserves your care and support. Do not act like your wife is ill-equipped to live life without you. She has gifts and abilities that you simply do not have, which she has been given for the good of your marriage. She deserves your involvement, so align your actions to that truth. Show her love through your care and honoring of her.

Realize your wife's significance with you in this life we have been given (Gen. 2:18–24). Consider this fact: A part of man was removed for the purpose of creating woman and at marriage a man is made complete once more. This does not mean that every man must get married, but it does mean that if a man remains single, a part of him will remain incomplete. The bottom line is this: Your wife is a critical part of God's plan for your life. Choose wisely who that woman will be and live remembering how significant she is.

Because of the union created in marriage, your relationship with your wife is part of your spiritual life. Refuse to live in disunity and unforgiveness with your wife, as this will tragically affect your spiritual life. A man cannot be in right relationship with God when he is not in right relationship with his wife. A man cannot experience the blessings of God when he is at odds with his wife.

We all want to live well. We all want to have good homes, strong families, and faithful children. We want to be a light for and path to the gospel for those around us. These things are made possible when wives and husbands live biblically in marriage: when wives submit to the authority of their husbands, just as Christ submitted to the authority of the Father and against His own desires went to the cross; when husbands submit to the need of their wives just as Christ submitted to our need when He suffered and died for our sins. Remember, as you struggle against your selfish, sinful, self and its desires, that your marriage relationship is a physical manifestation of the gospel to a world that is in desperate need of proof that hope can be found in Christ.

?≡   **Responding to God's Word in our lives:**

- Is your marriage relationship following a biblical pattern?

- Husband, how are you giving of yourself sacrificially for your wife?

- Wife, how are you trusting the Lord while being obedient to your husband?

- After considering these things, are there some areas of repentance needed in your marriage life (be specific)?

- After considering these things, should you go to your spouse and seek forgiveness for living life according to your own ways rather than the expectations of Jesus?

14

Living Well Together in a Difficult Place

1 Peter 3:8–12:
Finally, all of you, have unity of mind, sympathy, brotherly love, a tender heart, and a humble mind. (9) Do not repay evil for evil or reviling for reviling, but on the contrary, bless, for to this you were called, that you may obtain a blessing. (10) For whoever desires to love life and see good days, let him keep his tongue from evil and his lips from speaking deceit; (11) let him turn away from evil and do good; let him seek peace and pursue it. (12) For the eyes of the Lord are on the righteous, and his ears are open to their prayer. But the face of the Lord is against those who do evil.

When I was a very small child (I think about eight years old), my dad was transitioning from one ministry to another and we needed a place to live. The place available to us was a single-wide trailer with two small bedrooms. One of those bedrooms was used for my parents and the other was the home for my brother, two sisters, and me. It was a tight situation, to say the least. A full-size bed ran one direction and was used by my sisters. There was a narrow walkway to the side and at the end of the full-size bed a set of bunkbeds. This trailer was a very small living space, but I remember liking it despite the difficulties. We enjoyed our time there because my parents were determined to make this situation work for us. I think this sort of determination is missing from the relationships of many believers today. When we find ourselves in difficult situations, we think it is easier to change the situation than it is to make that situation work. Maybe if we did not have an easy way out, we would do what it takes to make the situation work and find ourselves stronger together for it.

Putting aside individual situations, understand that every believer living in this world, even though separate from this world in ideology and lifestyle, is expected to live among other believers with certain characteristics.

First, we have those things which are added to the character of believers living and working together. Disciples are surrendered to the design and desire of the one they follow. What is a mark of unified believers (Eph. 4:1–8)? Unity of mind arises when we are living as one global organism established and gifted by Christ for His purposes. This unified thinking removes self-exaltation and creates an eagerness to work together. It also causes each part (each individual) to see how they can contribute to the whole and manifests itself in a concern for missions, other churches, like-minded organizations, and other believers. A sure sign of a nonunified body of "believers" is a self-promoting ideology and inward thinking, because the unified body of Christ is always thinking beyond its own walls.

What is the process of creating a church of unified believers (Eph. 4:11)? Unified thinking is the result of hearts and minds prepared through the teaching of Scripture by biblically qualified men. The apostles established the foundation through the proclamation, writing, and teaching of the Scriptures. The prophets prepared the way and hope for our future as ones who spoke for God, primarily through their pronouncement of warnings and things to come. The evangelist is surrendered to reaching lost souls for Christ. The shepherd is equipped to endure the difficulties encountered during the developmental stages of believers. The teacher proclaims with clarity the realities of Scripture. Elders who have been gifted in teaching and evangelism are not simply managers or businessmen.

Note that God did not call businessmen to lead the church. God does not expect those men leading a church to expand an organization. God does expect those men to come alongside believers to encourage, teach, train, and disciple them so they may take the message of Christ to a lost and dying world. Then God grows the church locally and universally.

What is the end goal of this heart and mind preparation (Eph. 4:12–16)? A strong, healthy, mature body of individuals who are not tempted by every new fad, who build each other up, and shine a light of hope into a dark and dying world. As a body, we keep watch over one another's souls (Jude 20–23). We live life together, hurt together, rejoice together, and struggle together. We even face temptation together. We care for one another with a unified mind, hoping for all what Christ hopes for them: that they would come to repentance and pursue holiness rather than uncleanness.

Disciples of Christ have a capacity for entering into or sharing in the feelings or interests of others (Rom. 12:15). In fact, disciples love the body of Christ in the same way that a person loves his or her family. It is a strange relationship we have with our families. You may want to kill them yourself sometimes, but you will defend them against others even if it endangers your own life. When we become part of a local church body, we are in it through the good, the bad, the ugly, and the wonderful. Disciples show one another compassion and do not think themselves greater than those around them.

Disciples do not react to difficult situations the way the world around us would react. Disciples do not seek revenge for the terrible things that other individuals have done to them. (Recasting the saying attributed to Confucius, Douglas Horton remarked, "While seeking revenge, dig two graves — one for yourself" [https://www.brainyquote.com/quotes/douglas_horton_108526]) Disciples do not slander those who have slandered them. Disciples bless those who have hurt them, endangered their reputations, and caused them harm.

Disciples understand that blessing those who hurt them, endanger their reputations, and cause them harm is their calling by Christ (2 Tim. 2:3–4). Disciples are seeking something beyond happiness, social status, and comfort (2 Tim. 2:10–13). They seek the salvation of souls and they seek to honor Christ.

?≡ Responding to God's Word in our lives:

- How important to you are the relationships you have with other believers?

- Do you function as if what is taking place in their church is as important as what is taking place in your own church?

- Are you living in sin when it comes to your relationship with other believers?

- If so, will you repent of those sins and seek forgiveness where needed?

- If so, will you give yourself to living among all believers in a way that encourages, strengthens, and promotes the glory of Christ Jesus?

15

Confidence While Suffering in a Difficult Place

1 Peter 3:13–17:

Now who is there to harm you if you are zealous for what is good? (14) But even if you should suffer for righteousness' sake, you will be blessed. Have no fear of them, nor be troubled, (15) but in your hearts honor Christ the Lord as holy, always being prepared to make a defense to anyone who asks you for a reason for the hope that is in you; yet do it with gentleness and respect, (16) having a good conscience, so that, when you are slandered, those who revile your good behavior in Christ may be put to shame. (17) For it is better to suffer for doing good, if that should be God's will, than for doing evil.

At the age of 27, I was diagnosed with a malignant neoendocrine tumor in the pancreas that was moving into my small intestine. In the next few months, I had most of my pancreas removed (along with other things), and since then I have had yearly testing because tumors still exist in what is left of my pancreas and seem to reappear wherever they like. I have had several tumors removed from my body so far. During one exam, a tumor was found in my small intestine and the doctors were unable to identify it through testing. We were preparing to have it removed and my wife said to me, "Chad, worst case scenario it's cancer and you have five years left. I think you can get a lot done in five years." She said this to encourage me in the sovereign hand of God so that I would be more focused on what God is doing than on the trouble I was having to face.

I have been well acquainted with suffering. Sickness, death, loss of friends and family have been a normal part of life for me. This should not be a surprise because, contrary to popular teaching today, suffering is a promise for every follower of Christ. Now, because suffering is something we expect in our lives while following Jesus, the only question left to answer is this: Will we trust God in that suffering, confident in His ability to use that suffering for good? Or will we waste it with our sin?

We know that the eyes of the Lord are on the righteous (1 Peter 3:12). Of course, this is not a righteousness we have earned (Matt. 3:20). Our righteous works compare to filthy rags (Isa. 64:6). We do not do good (Rom. 3:10–12). I am talking about the righteousness that has been established, maintained, and guaranteed by Christ (Rom. 5:17–21).

He hears the prayers of those whose hearts are turned to Him. It is not a heart given to God by our own good graces or doings (Jer. 17:9), but a heart possessed by God through His pursuit of us (Rom. 8:30). Understand this: We are made righteous by Christ, protected by Christ, and given an audience with the Father by Christ.

Because it is in Christ that all these things have been established, and because it is Christ who is watching over our good, then we cannot be harmed by anyone who is not more powerful than Christ (Col. 1:15–19; John 16:31). In other words, NOBODY!

For followers, disciples, and proclaimers of Christ, suffering is most probable, but those who suffer in Christ are living within His blessing. Do not be afraid to suffer or of those who cause suffering. Do not be anxious about things that will come. Instead, pursue what Christ desires with all your heart.

Be ready to deliver the gospel to anyone who inquires about your hope. Share the gospel with disciplined strength, honorably, and in such a way that it creates its own defense. Be ready to suffer as you share the gospel. It is better to suffer for doing good than to suffer for doing evil.

?≡   **Responding to God's Word in our lives:**

- If suffering is the means by which Christ will lead others to Himself, are you ready to embrace your suffering for that purpose?

- If because of your relationship with Jesus and the call to suffering that has followed means you will not enjoy the pleasures of life until heaven, will you still follow Him?

- Have you been following Christ conditionally, as He meets your expectations? Would you repent today and embrace whatever suffering must come so that Christ may be glorified in you?

- In what areas of your life are you following Jesus conditionally?

- How will you redirect your thinking in these areas?

16

Confidence in the Suffering Savior

1 Peter 3:18–22:

For Christ also suffered once for sins, the righteous for the unrighteous, that he might bring us to God, being put to death in the flesh but made alive in the spirit, (19) in which he went and proclaimed to the spirits in prison, (20) because they formerly did not obey, when God's patience waited in the days of Noah, while the ark was being prepared, in which a few, that is, eight persons, were brought safely through water. (21) Baptism, which corresponds to this, now saves you, not as a removal of dirt from the body but as an appeal to God for a good conscience, through the resurrection of Jesus Christ, (22) who has gone into heaven and is at the right hand of God, with angels, authorities, and powers having been subjected to him.

During one time in my ministry life, I was a hospice chaplain for a nonprofit. "Nonprofit" meant we did not turn anyone away because of their financial situation. My job was to go into any home that would accept a Christian pastor and pray for them, listen to them, encourage them, and hopefully share the gospel with them. One home that I remember with little fondness was shared by ten pit-bull dogs. Generously, the homeowner would keep nine of them in the garage during my visit, so I was only left to deal with the oldest female dog. As I was sitting on the couch listening to my client (a dear, sweet lady), the mother pit bull came and sat on the couch next to me, with her lower jaw sticking out and teeth showing. She nudged my hand as if to say, "pet me," so I began petting this intimidating creature. As I did so, I noticed little black specks that began crawling across my hand. Trying to ignore all of this, I continued to minister with the client, in a visit that lasted about thirty minutes. I casually left the home and drove out of sight down the road—and then stopped and began stripping down to the essential clothing, throwing the rest in the open truck bed. Thankfully, it was winter, so I counted on the cold weather killing all the fleas now riding in the back of my truck. I drove straight home, showered for an hour, and hoped that a situation like that one would never occur again.

In the difficult situations of ministering to others, we should remember that when we face suffering while doing good, we are united with Christ. Paul said he suffered the loss of all things and counted them as rubbish, in order that he would know Him and be found in Him; that he might know Christ and share in His sufferings, becoming like Him in his death.

The just were treated unjustly (Acts 3:13–15). Christ died as a substitute (1 Peter 2:24), and as a once-only, singular sacrifice (Heb. 9:24–26). He suffered while doing good (1 Peter 1:20).

Consider that in Jesus' suffering He:

- Made the way of salvation.

- Tore the veil in the temple.

- Ushers us into the presence of God.

- Has made grace accessible to us.

Many things were made possible through Jesus' total physical death and His restored spirit before God. Breath left the body. Blood and water spilled out on the ground. The body was prepared and laid in the tomb, where it remained for three days. There was the reception of Christ's spirit and the renewal of His spirit (the immaterial part) before the resurrection.

During this time window of three days, while Jesus was waiting for the time of His resurrection, He was not sleeping, being inactive, or without cause. There is no reason for us to think that the saints who have left this earth before us are in a holding pattern or sleep. They are actively involved as ministers of God until we join them in resurrection at the call of Christ. They have not become angels. They are saints of God, glorifying God, as spirits that are no longer plagued by the pull of sin and the flesh.

He proclaimed victory to demons in prison, not Hell (Rev. 20:11–15). These are the demons who were imprisoned by God for acts of rebellion against their creation and who were warned of impending doom which was coming to all the earth.

A rescue was provided in the days of Noah for all who believed God. There was a message of repentance and belief to which only eight people responded and those eight were saved in an ark prepared for their safety.

The way of salvation from the flood and the way of salvation through Christ are illustrations, both showing salvation based on faith. Getting in the ark showed they believed the ark had been prepared to save them from a flood. Baptism shows we believe Christ defeated death in the resurrection to bring us new life in Himself. Both acts show faith in what God has promised: one by getting on an ark and the other through baptism.

Baptism is the proclamation of our belief that after the resurrection Christ took his place as Lord over all in heaven and earth. We get baptized to illustrate our belief that Jesus as risen Lord has delivered us from death and will receive us into His kingdom forever. Because baptism is not the way of salvation, we act as if it is optional. However, baptism is what followers of Christ do. Those who believed the flood would come went into the ark showing their belief. Those who believe Jesus died and rose from the dead get baptized to show their belief. Baptism is a declaration of what Jesus has done for you. If you have accepted Jesus Christ as your Savior, you need to be baptized.

You need to make a declaration.

You need to get in the boat.

You need to show you believe.

? ☰ **Responding to God's Word in our lives:**

- As you minister to those around you in various ways, have you trusted that even if you suffer while doing those things it is worth it?

- Will you show those around you, through baptism, that you believe Jesus is the only means of salvation from the judgment of God that will come to this earth one day?

    - Who will you talk to about this?

    - When will you schedule a date to be baptized?

17
Growth Project

1 Peter 4:1–11:

Since therefore Christ suffered in the flesh, arm yourselves with the same way of thinking, for whoever has suffered in the flesh has ceased from sin, (2) so as to live for the rest of the time in the flesh no longer for human passions but for the will of God. (3) For the time that is past suffices for doing what the Gentiles want to do, living in sensuality, passions, drunkenness, orgies, drinking parties, and lawless idolatry. (4) With respect to this they are surprised when you do not join them in the same flood of debauchery, and they malign you; (5) but they will give account to him who is ready to judge the living and the dead. (6) For this is why the gospel was preached even to those who are dead, that though judged in the flesh the way people are, they might live in the spirit the way God does. (7) The end of all things is at hand; therefore be self-controlled and sober-minded for the sake of your prayers. (8) Above all, keep loving one another earnestly, since love covers a multitude of sins. (9) Show hospitality to one another without grumbling. (10) As each has received a gift, use it to serve one another, as good stewards of God's varied grace: (11) whoever speaks, as one who speaks oracles of God; whoever serves, as one who serves by the strength that God supplies—in order that in everything God may be glorified through Jesus Christ. To him belong glory and dominion forever and ever. Amen.

"Since we are surrounded by so great a cloud of witnesses" is how the writer of Hebrews ends the great memorial written about faithful saints of God who surrendered themselves to suffering so that we might receive salvation. This statement reaches into a practical part of human motivation. It is a simple reality that having examples of people who plunged in and got into the not-so-pleasant parts of work motivates us to do things we would not otherwise do. Soldiers follow a leader who will go into the battle with them. Athletes follow a leader who will not give up. Churches follow leaders who will work alongside them when there isn't a spotlight on them. We follow Jesus into suffering because He faced suffering on our behalf and that motivates us to suffer for the sake of others.

We know that Christ does not expect us to do something that He Himself was unwilling to do (1 Peter 3:18). We should prepare for suffering by having the same mindset as Christ (Heb. 12:3; Phil. 2:3–7). Christ suffered for us to deliver us from sin judicially, and so we live separated from sin practically (Ezek. 16:32–42). We were the adulterous wife, the ones who ran to our sin and desires and thus brought wrath upon ourselves.

Prepare for suffering by having the same mindset as Christ (Heb. 12:3; Phil. 2:3–7). Jesus stepped in and took the wrath upon Himself and thereby satisfied God. Through His sacrifice, Jesus healed the wound we created. Jesus made it possible for us to have a relationship with God again. He suffered to bring us back to God and made it possible for us to have a relationship with God again. Now we endure suffering ourselves while bringing others to Christ so that He may give them to God.

In our identification with Christ, we put off our human passions, to do instead what God wants us to do. What we want or desire personally is separated from our decision making. What God wants becomes our pursuit.

In our identification with Christ, we put aside the things that unbelievers want to do. Some of those things include pursuing personal desires without restraint and having an intense desire for those things belonging to others. Some succumb to the consumption of large amounts of alcoholic beverages and unrestrained drunkenness accompanied by immoral behavior by a group of individuals. These actions demonstrate a placement of *things* over God's desire for us.

The world around us does not understand our identification with Christ and our surrender to God's will, so they are often critical of the life we have chosen. Even though they do not understand, they will still face judgment. Both those who are still living and those who have died when Christ returns will face judgment. The reality of judgment based on our response to the gospel is true for both the living and the dead. There is a difference between how people judge and how God judges. People will judge according to their perception of life and how we live. God judges according to the Spirit within us. The judgment that takes place by humankind is going to end, whereas the judgment of God is eternal.

Keep a clear head; be sensible about the life you live and remain undistracted from prayer. Make living for God and unto others a priority. Love one another even when it is hard to do so. Be willing to sacrifice to care for or protect others from harm. Do this for each other and don't complain about it as if the sacrifice is too much. Use your gifts for the good of others. Use them because this is your place and calling as a steward of God's goodness toward men. If your gift is speaking, use it to communicate God's message and not your own. If your gift is service, use it as an outpouring and demonstration of what God is doing in you.

When we live for God unto others, Christ will be glorified by all we do.

When our lives, our families, and our churches glorify Christ, then and then alone is glory where it belongs.

?≡ **Responding to God's Word in our lives:**

- What pattern of life choices are you following?

- Are you living to fulfill your own dreams or passions?

- Are you living for the fulfillment of God's will through Christ Jesus in this world?

- Are you willing to lay aside your own dreams and passions for the sake of others?

- Are you willing to let Jesus take the glory for everything He does through you, even if you are never recognized yourself?

- If you have been living according to your own passions rather than those of Jesus, will you repent of that way of living today?

- How can you begin living in such a way that God's glory is always the desired outcome, rather than your own desires or glory?

- In what way can you begin leading others in that way of thinking from day to day?

18

Rejoicing When Life Is Hard

1 Peter 4:12–13:
Beloved, do not be surprised at the fiery trial when it come upon you to test you, as though something strange were happening to you. (13) But rejoice insofar as you share Christ's sufferings, that you may also rejoice and be glad when his glory is revealed.

Difficulties come and go. This has not really been a big deal to me. I like to be the guy who steps in and saves the day or completes a task that others would not be able to do. What I struggle with is when things that I have planned do not go the way I think they should. I struggle when investments I made do not turn out the way I thought they would. I struggle when I do not meet my own expectations. I struggle when I feel I have let my family down. I struggle when friends let me down. I struggle when a seemingly great day on Sunday turns into multiple criticisms on Monday.

The question for us is not how we will deal with situations that are difficult. The question is: How will we deal with those things that are seemingly impossible for us? Will those things drive us into Jesus' arms, reminding us that the sin-created brokenness of life is why Jesus died? Or will we allow the trials of this life and unmet expectations to turn us away from Jesus altogether?

In the end, if our expectation is that God is going to do great and marvelous things in *our* lives according to our definitions, and then He doesn't, we will look for those things elsewhere. Discouraged, we will abandon the faith. Disheartened, we will become apathetic. Distraught, we will set our sights on something else.

Life is full of hardship: death, pain, poverty, famine, disappointment. The work of the enemy increases that suffering in the life of the believer. Therefore, those who are in Christ should not be caught off guard by not expecting hardship. When God allows a purging event, development process, molding work, or difficult circumstance into your life, He is preparing you for His purposes (2 Cor. 12:10). Suffering for a follower of Christ is not an if, but a when. The reality for Christ followers is suffering (John 15:20). Those trials will affect your life and your plans (John 21:18).

Trials will show your faith or lack of it (1 Peter 1:6; Matt. 13:21). When these expected trials take place in our lives, we need to see them for what they are: They are God working in us and through us. They are God fulfilling His redemption plan in this world.

We know that trials will come and are a part of the battle. Trials prove our faith and grow us in Christlikeness.

So, we rejoice! We rejoice in suffering because as followers of Christ we have an identity with Christ. Our identity is in who we are suffering for (1 Thess. 2:19–20). Our identity is in how our suffering matters (Phil. 3:10). Our identity is in who we are suffering with (Heb. 13:5–6).

As followers of Christ, we hope in that which is to come. Part of our hope is the end of our suffering. We look forward to participating in the celebration which will be Christ's rule. We hope in the knowledge that He who has always been faithful, has been and will be faithful to us.

?☰ **Responding to God's Word in our lives:**

- Does suffering cause you to hold more closely to Jesus, or does it pull you away from Him?

- When you endure suffering, how do you rejoice in what God will do through that suffering?

- Is there an area in which you need to repent before Christ Jesus regarding your response to suffering?

- How will you respond to suffering in a way that brings glory to Jesus in the days ahead?

19

How We Suffer Matters

1 Peter 4:14–19:

If you are insulted for the name of Christ, you are blessed, because the Spirit of glory and of God rests upon you. (15) But let none of you suffer as a murderer or a thief or an evildoer or as a meddler. (16) Yet if anyone suffers as a Christian, let him not be ashamed, but let him glorify God in that name. (17) For it is time for judgment to begin at the household of God; and if it begins with us, what will be the outcome for those who do not obey the gospel of God? (18) And if the righteous is scarcely saved, what will become of the ungodly and the sinner?

(19) Therefore let those who suffer according to God's will entrust their souls to a faithful Creator while doing good.

When I was a child, one of my father's co-workers used to call me "Dennis the Menace." I earned that name because, though I think I was an easy kid to get along with according to my attitude, I just seemed to find myself in constant trouble. Often that trouble led to stitches or bumps and bruises. Once in a while I would ruin something of value to my parents by trying to make it better or using things in ways they were not designed to be used.

One day in particular I was watching my dad burn some material in a pit behind my house — a pit that had been created for burning material after our house burned down (I was not home when that incident happened). Before the fire was completely burnt out, my dad had to leave and instructed me to stay away from the pit and "do not throw anything else in it." Well, I determined that I should help, and after he left, I began loading the fire with material again. Suddenly, a wind came blowing across the field and some of the burning material flew at me and caught my hands on fire. I spent the rest of the summer with bandages on my hands, and still have some scars today. That long summer of pain and suffering was a natural consequence of my poor decisions.

When we begin talking about suffering in the name of Christ Jesus, we must separate the natural consequences of our sinful or foolish decisions with those things that happen because we are following Jesus. When we suffer for making bad decisions, we cannot claim martyrdom; we just have to face the consequences. When we suffer for doing exactly what the Lord has asked us to do, then we bring glory to God in the way we suffer. When that happens, remember that our Lord endured insults too.

There may be times in your life when you face criticism and mockery for your faith in Christ. When that happens, remember that you do not have to be afraid of men (Is. 51:4–7). Remember that our Lord was not accepted by religious leaders (John 7:47–52). The Jews accused Jesus of harboring a demon (John 8:48). Even when He did the impossible, Jesus was written off as nothing (John 9:28–34).

If you are mocked, criticized, and disregarded for following Christ, you are blessed. Blessed because the glory of Christ awaits you. Blessed because the Spirit of God is within you.

It is honorable and blessed to suffer for Christ's sake; just don't suffer for being sinful. There is nothing blessed about facing persecution for being an arrogant, hateful individual. There is nothing blessed about being mocked or punished when you take from others for dishonest gain. Those who face suffering for the evil acts they commit are not honored by God for that suffering. Those who face trouble because they cannot mind their own business bring trouble upon themselves.

What if you suffer for living the way Christ has instructed and declaring what Christ has declared? Do not bring shame to Christ in the way you suffer: *"Let him not be ashamed."* Suffer in a way that glorifies Christ. Suffer in a way that makes His name great. Suffer believing that God is in control. Suffer believing that God is using this for good (Phil. 1:12–14).

Be assured of this: Not all suffering in a follower of Christ stems from persecution. God will bring suffering into the life of His children when they are disobedient to Him, to bring them back into obedience. God will bring suffering into the life of those who reject the gospel to bring them to salvation. God will not allow sin to continue in the life of any individual. At some point, there will be a price for sinful choices.

Those who are suffering because of sin should repent rather than seeking comfort. Those who suffer because they are obedient to Christ should trust that they are safe in the Creator's care and continue in the way of Christ.

Suffering is going to take place in this life. Let's not suffer for living a selfish, disobedient life. Let's suffer while doing good and suffer well when it happens. Let's suffer in such a way that the world around us is made to recognize Christ. Let's suffer in such a way that Christ is lifted above our own pleasure. Let's suffer in such a way that even those who cause our suffering may one day be brought to Christ.

?≡ Responding to God's Word in our lives:

- Are you able to discern why you are suffering today?

  - Is it because of natural consequences?

  - Is it because of sin?

- Is it because of persecution as a result of living for Jesus?

- If it is a natural consequence of sin or foolishness, are you confronting the decisions made which put you in that position and living in wisdom moving forward?

- If it is sin, have you repented of that sin and reestablished your way unto the Lord?

- If it is persecution as a result of living for Jesus, are you allowing the suffering to consume you, or are you trusting Jesus to continue using you even during the suffering?

20

God's Caregivers in Suffering

1 Peter 5:1–4:

So I exhort the elders among you, as a fellow elder and a witness of the suffering of Christ, as well as a partaker in the glory that is going to be revealed: (2) shepherd the flock of God that is among you, exercising oversight, not under compulsion, but willingly, as God would have you; not for shameful gain, but eagerly; (3) not domineering over those in your charge, but being examples to the flock. (4) And when the chief Shepherd appears, you will receive the unfading crown of glory.

Most of the time I think the modern church has lost an understanding of what an "elder" is. We treat them as though they are individuals put in a board/leadership position for a set time and then they are done. We act as though their impact upon us is minimal. We treat them as if they are just people whom we had to have so the constitutional number was met.

The truth is that they are so much more than that. Elders (which include the pastor(s)) are called by God to a lifetime commitment as God's caretakers for the church. They teach, lead, and invest themselves in the church body as part of their responsibility. They also defend the faith and protect the church from harm. Peter says they guide us in the way we should go when we are not sure what way that is (John 10:11–18).

Peter's request in chapter 5 is addressed to older, mature individuals: leaders in the church of Christ. He earnestly appeals for your action in the lives of those whom God has given you while enduring suffering.

Peter speaks as one who participates in the role of elder in his church. He speaks as one who watched Christ suffer during His ministry and while going to and hanging on the cross. He saw the fulfillment of God's plan in the resurrection and ascension of Christ. He speaks as a fellow believer waiting for the return of Christ.

Peter gives elders instructions to follow: Care for the church that God has placed under your authority. Concentrate on the direction and work happening in your own house. Do not involve yourself in the affairs of other churches.

He goes on to give examples of shepherding (Ps. 23). Show the sheep where to find food and provide a place of rest for them. Direct them into safe places. Be a presence of restoration to the soul. Lead them in a life of holy living that Christ may be glorified in them. Guard them from those who would hurt, destroy, and mislead them. Stand with them when evil confronts them. Most importantly, direct them to the source of eternal joy and peace.

In order to do these things, pay attention to the lives of people in your church — not because someone makes you do it, but because you desire to do it. It is not done for your personal glory, but because there is nothing you would rather do. You don't do this with an iron fist, as though somehow you are judge over them. Instead, lead them with your teaching of the Word and your life before God and them (1 Tit. 4:12–16).

Be an example to them in:

- Your conversation.

- The way you act.

- The love you have for others.

- Faith centered in Christ our King.

- Living a life that does not ruin the good things God has given us.

- Teaching them the Word of God.

- Giving time to the care of and practice of the spiritual gift God has given you.

- Examining your life and your teaching carefully.

Determine that these are good, honorable ways to spend your life for your own self and the sake of those for whom you are caring. The life of an elder is surrendered to the care of God's people until Christ's return, and the glorification of Christ in His return is the singular thing that drives an elder.

?≡ Responding to God's Word in our lives:

- If you are an elder in your church, are you caring for those people God has given you through suffering?

  - Guiding them to respond biblically.

  - Praying for them.

  - Making yourself available to them.

- If you are not an elder in your church, are you placing yourself under the care of the elders in suffering?

  - Opening up to them about the things you are facing.

  - Listening to their instruction.

  - Seeking their care in prayer for you.

21

Humility Is Key to Living Together in a Difficult Place

1 Peter 5:5–7:

Likewise, you who are younger, be subject to the elders. Clothe yourselves, all of you, with humility toward one another, for God opposes the proud but gives grace to the humble.

(6) Humble yourselves, therefore, under the mighty hand of God so that at the proper time he may exalt you, (7) casting all your anxieties on him, because he cares for you.

The practice of humility is a very difficult thing. It includes seeking forgiveness from God when we have sinned against Him; seeking forgiveness from our spouses when we have sinned against them; seeking forgiveness from our children when we have sinned against them.

I remember a time when I was determined to get a job done and I was not willing to admit I couldn't do it on my own. We had a basement refrigerator and the kitchen fridge died. So, I decided I could get the fridge from the basement to the kitchen with just the help of a dolly. Long story made short: the dolly straps came off and the dolly fell off in the middle of the procedure. I was stuck on the stairway myself holding this refrigerator. Tracy, my wife, came to the stairway door and said, "What are you going to do now?" Did I mention she had instructed me to ask a neighbor friend to help before I began this task? Replying to herself, she said, "Well, I guess I will have to help you with it." She grabbed the top end of the refrigerator and pulled as I pushed from the bottom, one step at a time to the top of the stairs. Exhausted—but with the refrigerator in the kitchen—I begin to humbly seek forgiveness and praise her for saving me from a jam created by my pride. I learned once again that my way is not always the right way.

Maturity in the body of Christ comes through surrender to God's ways. Maturity is not optional. If we do not mature in our faith, we will be unstable, uncertain, and easily manipulated (Eph. 4:13–14). Maturity is the goal for every follower of Jesus (Col. 1:28). Maturity in the faith is Christlike (Luke 2:52). Maturing believers draw in unbelievers (Acts 9:31). This is not transfer growth. This is new believers coming to faith in Christ.

Being subject to those whom God has given to care for the church (elders) is an opportunity for you to show subjection to God and allows you to grow in faith (1 Peter 5:1–4). They are the physical representation of Christ to you. They are the shepherds of God and the guides to maturity. They are the examples that can be followed (Phil. 3:12–17).

Cooperation in the body of Christ comes through humility. Every believer — elders, deacons, men, women, children, young and old, mature in the faith and young in the faith — must have an attitude of humility toward others. The arrogant individual can lead others to wrong actions (Prov. 10:17). The Christian hope is not for personal superiority, but for others to see what God can do in a life surrendered to Him (Matt. 5:16). Personal ambition cannot be part of a believer's life; rather, we must place the good of others before our own privileges or desires (Phil. 2:3).

God's working in the body of Christ comes through humility, which has a reasonable purpose. God works against those who are arrogant, but God works within the life of the humble. If we are consumed with our own lives and/or judgments, God will oppose us. If we humbly submit our lives to God for the good of others, His grace will provide more than we deserve as individuals or as a church.

Humility in the body of Christ manifests itself in surrender of everything to God.

A logical conclusion is to determine to let God have His way with your life. Let God decide when to exalt you. Give God the cares and pressures of your life. Do these things knowing that God desires your good.

?≡ **Responding to God's Word in our lives:**

- Do you believe God is more concerned about what is good for you than you are?

- Do you believe God is able to be judge over those things that you see as imperfections in the lives of others, so that you do not have to?

- Are you willing to let God do whatever He wants with your life?

- Are you willing to let God do whatever He wants in the lives of those around you?

- Are you willing to let God exalt you instead of exalting yourself?

- Do you need to repent of anything in the area of not living humbly before God and man?

- Is there someone from whom you should be seeking forgiveness?

22

God's Glory in a Difficult Place

1 Peter 5:8–11:

Be sober-minded; be watchful. Your adversary the devil prowls around like a roaring lion, seeking someone to devour. (9) Resist him, firm in your faith, knowing that the same kinds of suffering are being experienced by your brotherhood throughout the world. (10) And after you have suffered a little while, the God of all grace, who has called you to his eternal glory in Christ, will himself restore, confirm, strengthen, and establish you. (11) To him be the dominion forever and ever. Amen.

One of my closest friends while I was growing up lived on a small hobby farm. His dad raised their beef, and as a result they always had a large bull on the property, behind a tall fence threaded with an electric wire. If we stayed out of the cows' living space, the fence created a place of protection for us. Because we were young boys and I had a taste for adventure, we would sometimes run through the cows' living space, hoping to get to the other side without the bull catching up to us. This was not a wise game for us to play. I am certain that the games we play when it comes to our spiritual lives may have even greater consequences for us than angering a captive bull.

Many considerations go into accomplishing the tasks before us. We need to be light and life to a dying world. We should strengthen and encourage one another in the faith. We are called to live well in a world that is opposed to what we hold dear. It is also important to develop disciples who will faithfully carry on when we are gone.

We must be self-restrained when tempted to be anxious about life. Remember, anxiety never makes things better (Matt. 6:25–34). Anxiety manifests a flesh-controlled life when we should be trusting in God (Phil. 4:4–8). This is not a "don't worry, be happy" attitude: God will fix my car, clean my house, give me the answers to the test, raise my children, maintain my checkbook, write my sermon. Instead, being sober-minded is a controlled way of trusting God while continuing to obediently care for our areas of responsibility.

Our job is to prepare ourselves to do what must be done when the time comes for us to do it, such as a soldier in a watchtower. Grow in knowledge of the Truth (2 Tim. 3:16–17): not intellectual understanding (2 Tim. 3:7), but intimate understanding which leads to wisdom and discernment (2 Tim. 3:14). Weaponize your mind for battle (Ps. 119:11).

You may be wondering why the believer has to be so diligent. It is because we are being hunted. We intellectually know the devil is our enemy even when he acts like he is our friend. Even those who act as though he is an enemy can forget how fierce and relentless he is. He is the deadliest of all created beings. We tremble, have nightmares, protect our children from mass murderers, serial killers, mad men. We forget that they are nothing in comparison to the devil who seeks to ruin our lives (both terrestrial and eternal). Knowing that he has lost, he desperately seeks anyone whom he can take with him to Hell.

The hunter is obsessed with your destruction. Satan is not satisfied with wounding his prey: Satan seeks to ruin, destroy, leave nothing good to those in his sights.

Do not allow him easy access to your life. Place yourself on steady ground. The foundation of your life must be strong and indestructible. The foundation must be Christ Jesus—not religion, nor heroes, nor family. Jesus and Jesus alone will never fail.

Understand the scope of this war taking place in the lives of believers everywhere. Be part of the stronghold of saints. Stand firm against the enemy. Do not give him room to win (Heb. 12:1).

Embrace the reality of suffering and endure for now. Life is short, it is a vapor, our suffering will end. Believe that God's grace will be sufficient (2 Cor. 12:7–10). Believe that He sought you, He bought you, He saved you from sin and death, He has already secured for you a place in eternity, He will never let you go. He will make you the way He created you to be and will give you the ability to accomplish that purpose He has called you to. He will develop in you a firm resolve and unshakeable faith, and will anchor you in the foundation of truth. When our time is over here in this place, we will give God the glory for what He has done and proclaim that for us it has been good to be near God (Ps. 73:23–28).

?≡ **Responding to God's Word in our lives:**

- How are you preparing for your involvement in the ongoing war for the souls of men?

- How are you living as if your preparedness to endure the enemies of Christ Jesus matters?

- What are you doing so that in and through you Christ will be glorified when the devil seeks to stomp out the work Christ is doing in you?

23

There Is Only One Life of Grace

1 Peter 5:12–14:

By Silvanus, a faithful brother as I regard him, I have written briefly to you, exhorting and declaring that this is the true grace of God. Stand firm in it. (13) She who is at Babylon, who is likewise chosen, sends you greetings, and so does Mark, my son. (14) Greet one another with the kiss of love. Peace to all of you who are in Christ.

Grace living is trusting that God has everything under control. You are right where God wants you to be. You are correctly positioned for obedience to Jesus Christ so that you or others may be saved. You are surrounded by the gracious gifts which only God can give during your struggle.

Grace living is placing your faith in what God is doing beyond the struggle. You have a hope that goes beyond the struggle. You have a resurrection that has been guaranteed by Christ. You have an inheritance that cannot be taken away. The trials may be hard, but they are only causing you to look more passionately for the return of Christ. They are causing you to want more than this life can give. They are developing in you a thirst for God. They remind you that things are not the way they are supposed to be, but they will be some day.

Grace living is a willingness to suffer so that others may know of Christ. It is a life beyond yourself, lived for those who will come after us. It is a surrender to give of ourselves now so that many will enjoy the hope ahead of us.

The life of grace surrenders to what Jesus has made complete on the cross and pursues a life of obedience from a grateful heart. The grace life:

- Is determined to kill the flesh-driven desire of life before grace.

- Is an insatiable desire for more of Christ.

- Rests in Christ as the foundation for salvation, strength, protection, and life.

- Embraces the role of ambassador to the world of God's great mercy toward us.

- Sacrifices everything for the sake of the gospel.

- Subjects itself to ruling authorities as God's governors in this world.

- Embraces the opportunity to trust God with the outcome of our good work among unjust employers.

- Provides a wife the strength to submit to her husband as head of the home while he submits himself to the needs of his family.

- Calls individuals to put aside their own rights and mercifully forgive those who have hurt them.

- Is a life of confidence while suffering because of the hope we have in Christ Jesus.

- Responds to suffering in obedience as exemplified by Christ.

- Is lived in a focused effort to do the will of God over our own will.

- Finds joy in the midst of trials.

- Allows us to suffer well.

- Is encouraged by the presence of persons whom God has given for our care.

- Is humbled by God's goodness to someone so wretched as oneself.

- Is lived carefully for the glory of the One who has made us free.

?☰ Responding to God's Word in our lives:

- Have you believed in Jesus for salvation?

- Have you repented of your sins for which He died?

- Are you living in new life through the power of His resurrection?

- If you have believed in Jesus for salvation,

    - In what way are you living like He has changed and is changing you?

    - In what way are you trusting Him to take care of your material things as you live to glorify Him with every moment of your life?

- Are you under the care of a church family that is investing itself in the continual work of Christ for your good and His glory?

Other Titles from Grace Acres Press

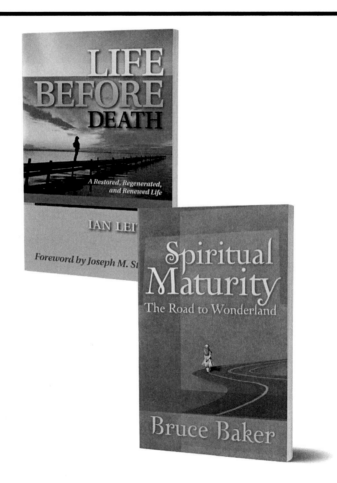

AVAILABLE AT GRACEACRESPRESS.COM

OR WHEREVER BOOKS ARE SOLD.

Other Titles from Grace Acres Press

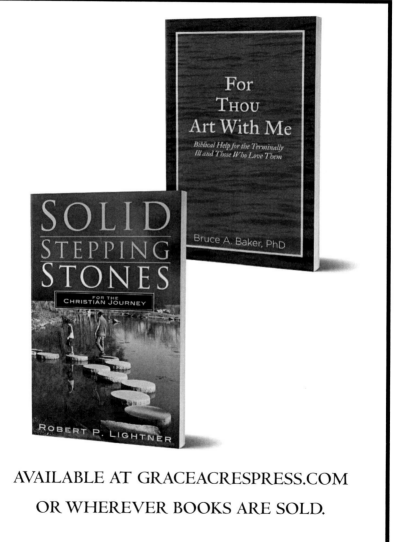

AVAILABLE AT GRACEACRESPRESS.COM
OR WHEREVER BOOKS ARE SOLD.